COLOURSUTRA

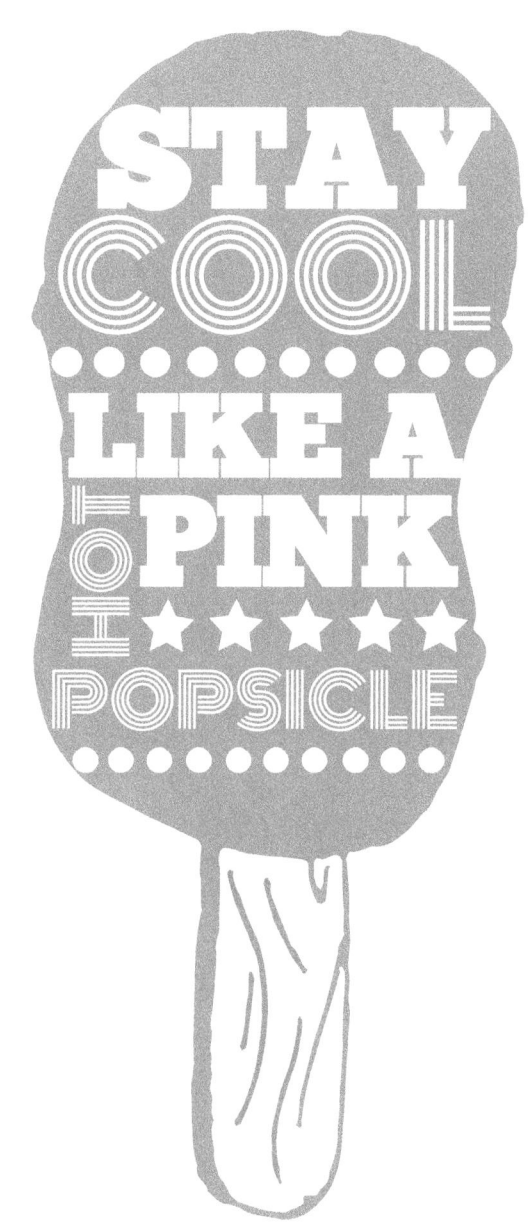

STAY COOL LIKE A PINK POPSICLE

HOT

Food

Colouring Book For Adults

The Ultimate Stress Reliever

Created by Sofy Rahman

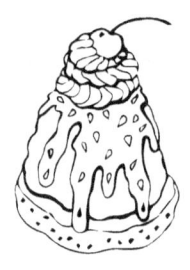

ABOUT SOFY

HAVING SPENT 7 YEARS AS A FLIGHT ATTENDANT,
SOFY WAS HEAVILY INSPIRED BY THE REMNANTS
OF ANCIENT CARTHAGE WHICH LEFT ITS MARK FROM
THE BAY OF TUNIS TO THE VIBRANT STREET LIFE OF LA RAMBLA
IN THE HEART OF BARCELONA.

HER LOVE FOR WANDERLUST ADVENTURES AND HER ZEST FOR LIFE
HAS LED HER TO UNFORGETTABLE JOURNEYS;
FROM BEING CHOSEN TO PARTICIPATE IN THE
MRS SINGAPORE PAGEANT TO WINNING AWARDS FOR HER DESIGN
WORK.

SHE FINALLY CLIPPED HER WINGS IN 2014
TO START HER OWN BRANDIN G AND MARKETING AGENCY.

SHE BELIEVES THAT NO ONE SHOULD EVER FORGET THE JOY OF
COLOURING AND THAT
SIMPLICITY MAKES FOR LESS STRESS AND MORE HAPPINESS.

WWW.SOFYSTUFF.COM

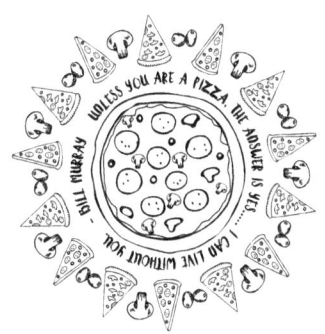

BEFORE I START WITH MY SUPER LONG DEDICATION,
I WOULD LIKE TO
SAY A HUGE THANKS TO EVERYONE WHO HAS BOUGHT
COLOURSUTRA'S FIRST BOOK.

THAT FEELING I GET WHEN I SEE FELLOW
COLOURSUTRISTS RELIVING THEIR CHILDHOOD ALL OVER
AGAIN IS UNDOUBTEDLY PRICELESS.
KEEP THOSE CREATIVE JUICES FLOWING!
ALWAYS A JOY TO SEE THE DRAWINGS COMING ALIVE.

ONCE AGAIN, MY HEARTFELT THANKS TO MY HUSBAND,
MY PARENTS, MY MUM IN LAW,
MY FAMILY AND CLOSE FRIENDS.

NO WORDS CAN DESCRIBE HOW GRATEFUL AND THANKFUL
FOR ALL OF YOUR SUPPORT AND WORDS OF
ENCOURAGEMENT.

YOU ARE THE INSPIRATION (ON TOP OF MY LOVE FOR FOOD)
THAT I HAVE DECIDED TO CREATE
COLOURSUTRA'S SECOND BOOK.
THIS BOOK IS MUCH MORE FUN, YUMMIER AND HOPEFULLY
IT BRINGS MORE JOY TO ALL OF YOU!

HAPPY COLOURING!

LOVE ,

Sofy

Introduction

Have you always wanted to find a way to destress? If so, you are not alone.

Colour therapy is one of the most popular methods of relaxation at the moment.

Couple that with some soothing music, and you will find that it can be extremely enriching.

When was the last time you actually held a colour pencil, and let it flow

 across a clean white page?

Growing up, I was introduced to the joy of art classes at the tender age of 5.

Oh the joy of colouring and drawing with oil pastels, coloured pencils and other

medium!

Honestly , I lost touch with my creative side when I was at the peak of my youth as other

distractions and interests entered my life.

 As I got older, experiences I gained from frequent travelling, further inspired me

to reconnect with my creative self, propelling me to produce the designs in this book.

No one can deny the therapeutic effect colouring can have on one's well being;

in fact it can even soothe the savage beast!

I found that colour therapy really helped me in more ways than one.

Apart from the many colouring books available out there, why not challenge yourself to

this book?

It offers a 50-day challenge to complete all 50 designs.

As simple as that!

When we put our minds into completing a page a day,

we not only destress ourselves and improve our colouring,

but we also exercise - it disciplines us.

So , are you ready to take up this 50 day challenge with me?

Come join me and the rest of the Coloursutra community on Facebook today!

https://www.facebook.com/groups/coloursutra/

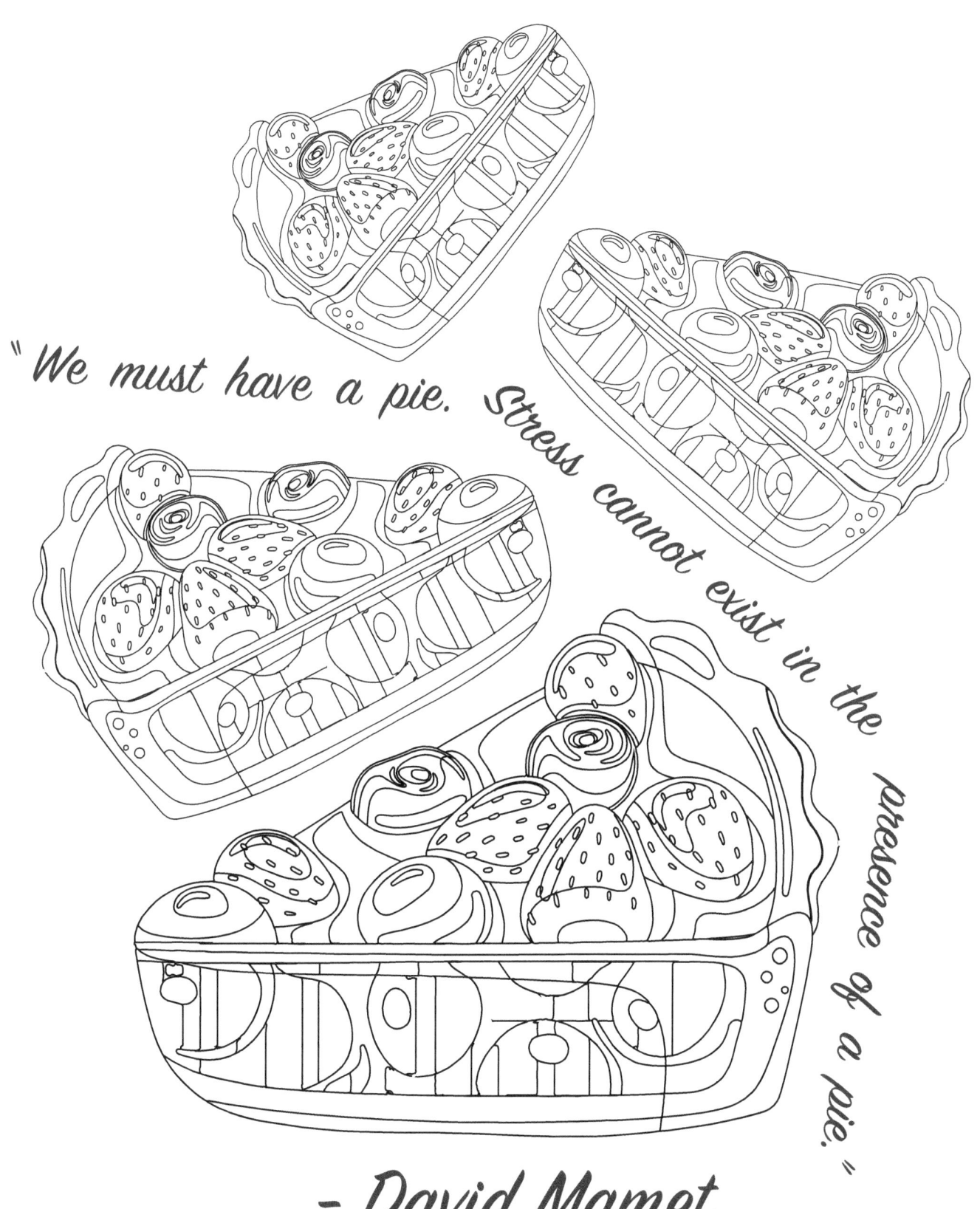

"We must have a pie. Stress cannot exist in the presence of a pie."

- David Mamet

Between the optimist and the pessimist,
the difference
is droll.

- Oscar Wilde

The optimist
sees the doughnut,
the pessimist ... the hole!

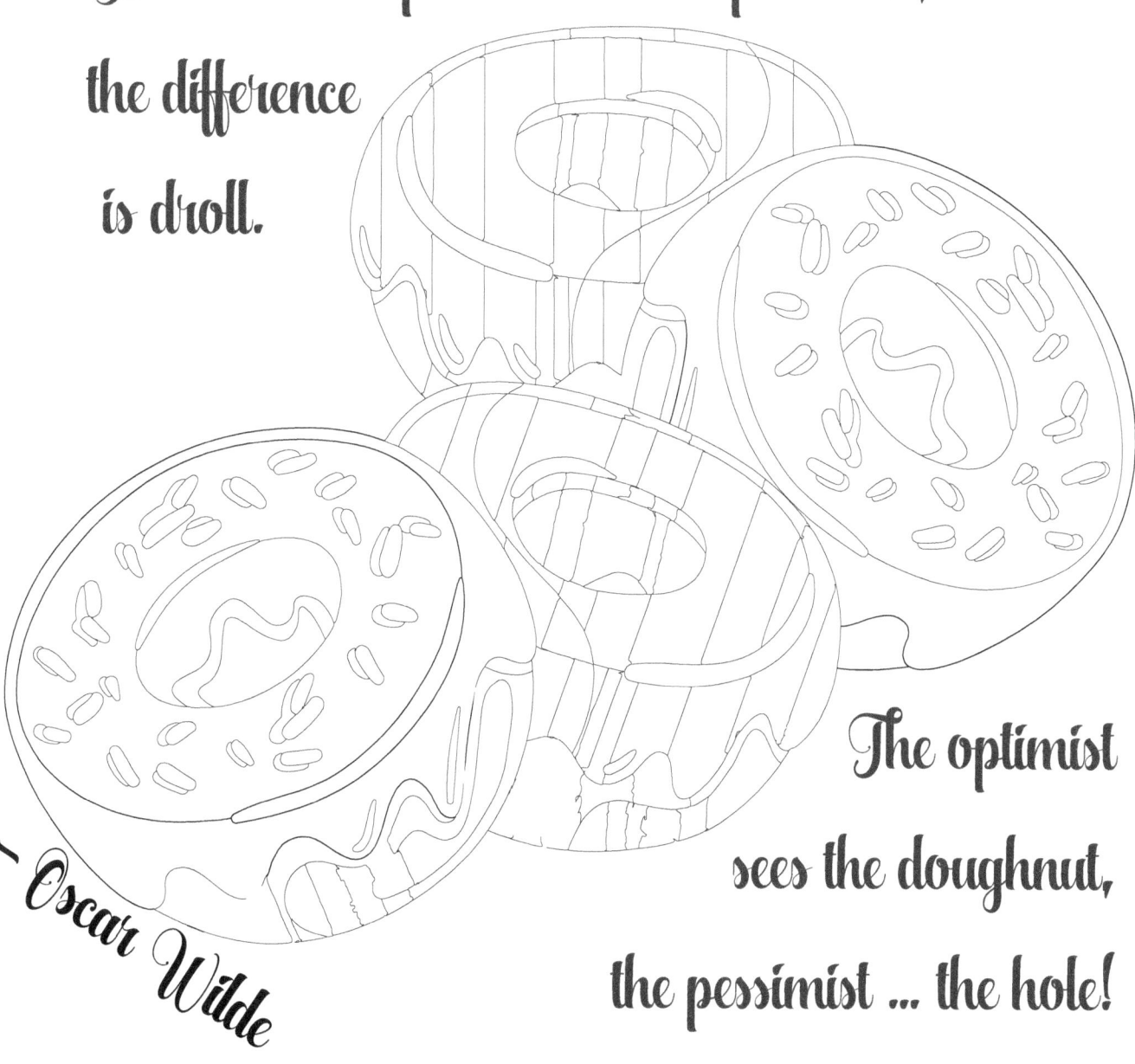

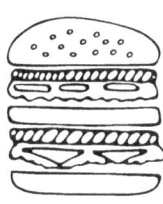

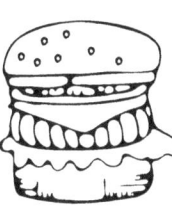

IF IT'S FLIPPING HAMBURGERS
AT MCDONALD'S,
BE THE BEST HAMBURGER
FLIPPER
IN THE WORLD.
WHATEVER IT IS YOU DO,
YOU HAVE TO
MASTER YOUR CRAFT.
- SNOOP DOGG

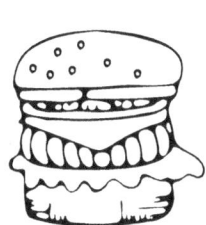

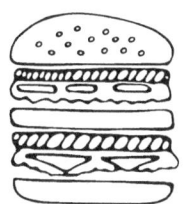

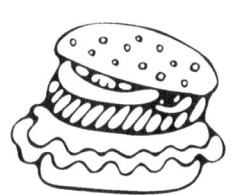

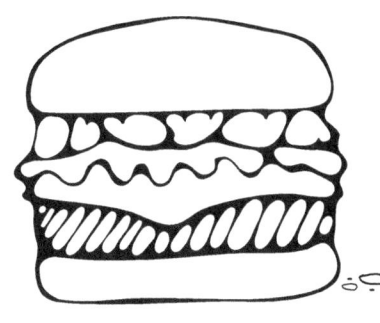

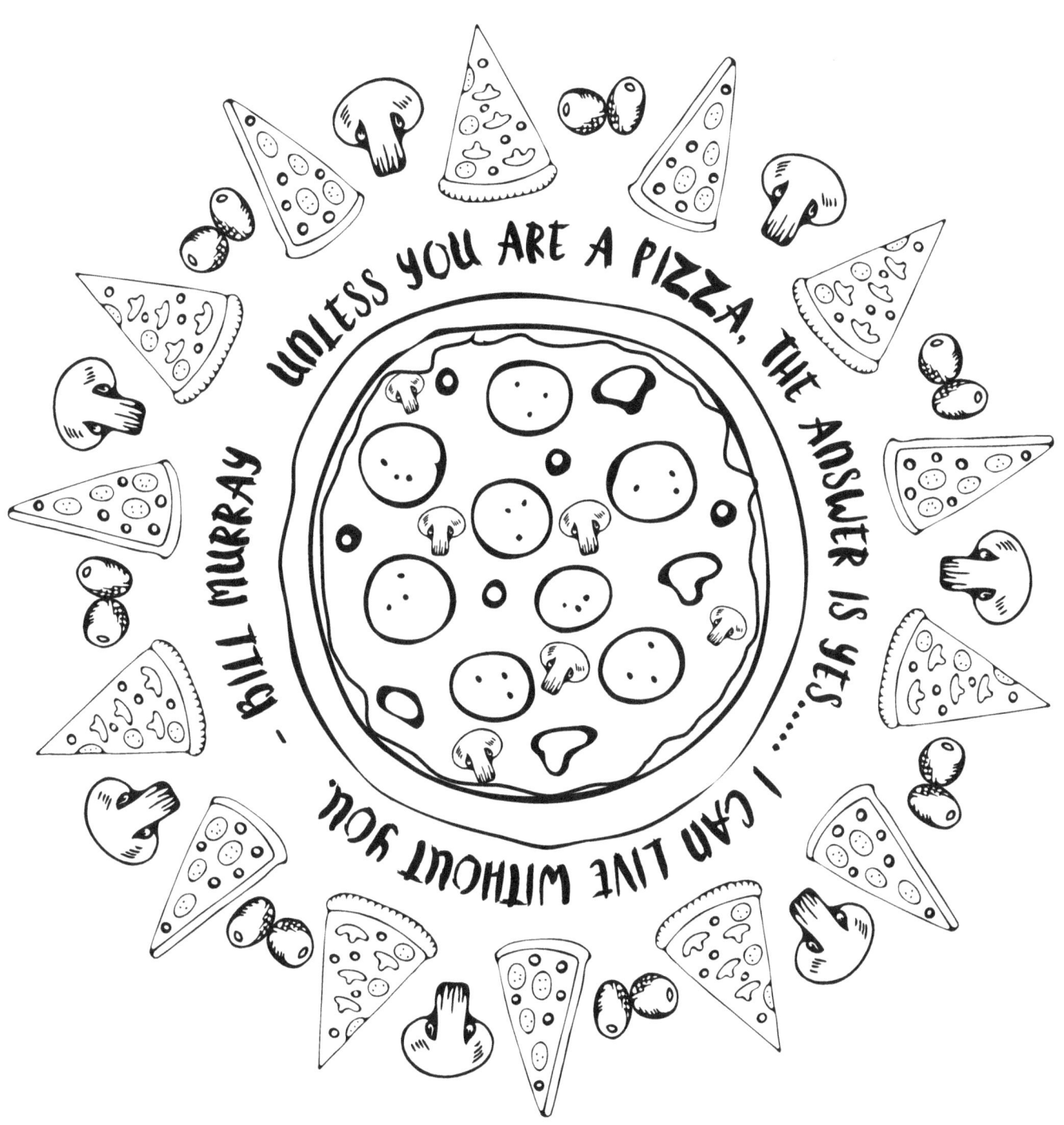

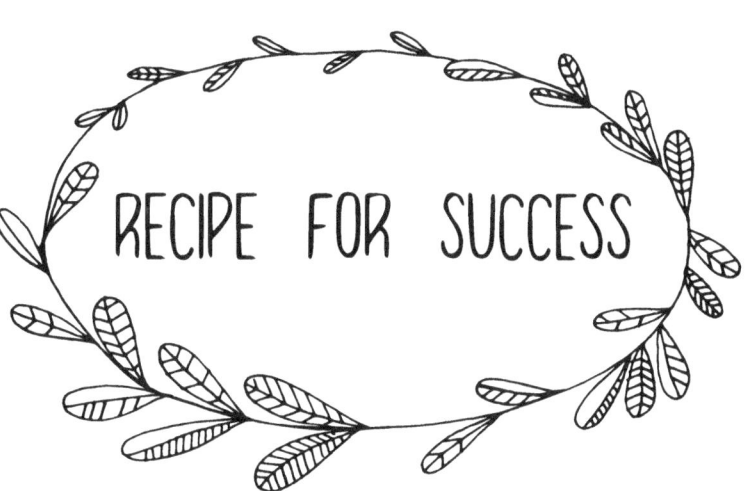

RECIPE FOR SUCCESS

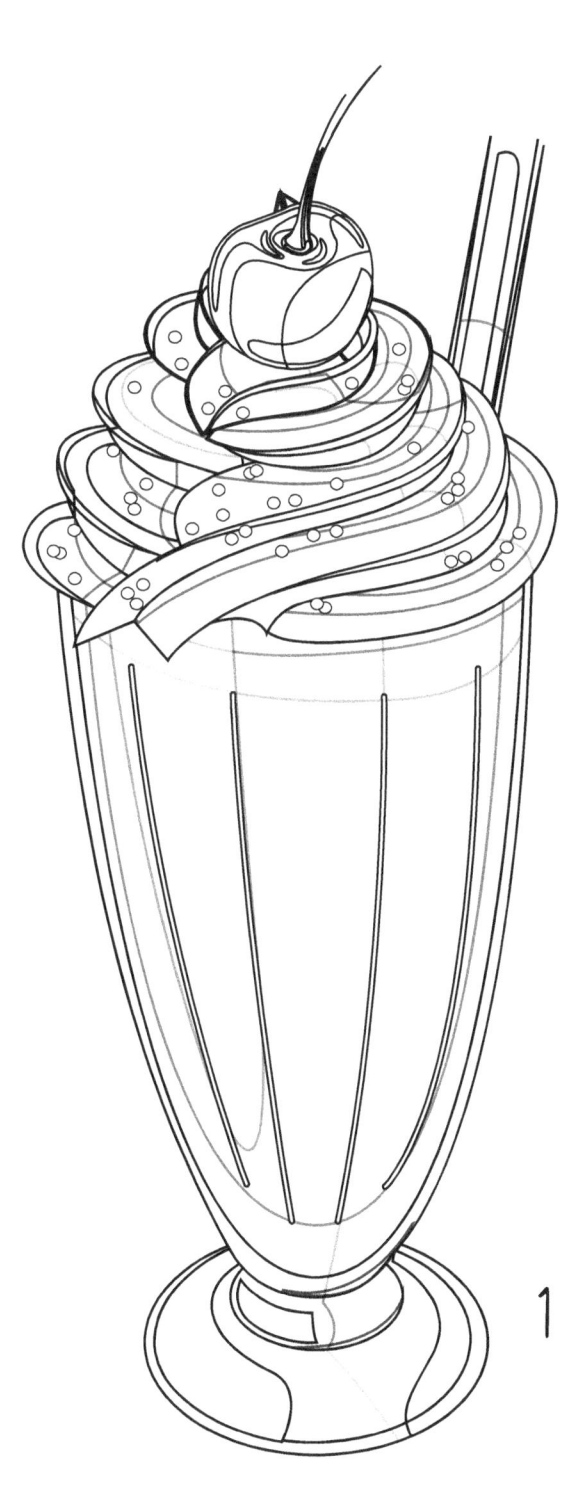

INGREDIENTS:

2 CUPS OF EFFORT

2 CUPS OF KINDNESS

1 HANDFUL OF CURIOUSITY

3 TABLESPOONS OF HONESTY

2 CUPS OF TEAMWORK

2 CUPS OF IMAGINATION

1 CUP OF EXCITEMENT

1 HANDFUL OF FAIRNESS

1 SPRINKLE OF PRIDE IN YOUR WORK

* NOTE: SUCCESS IS ALWAYS BETTER
WHEN SHARED SO PASS IT AROUND!

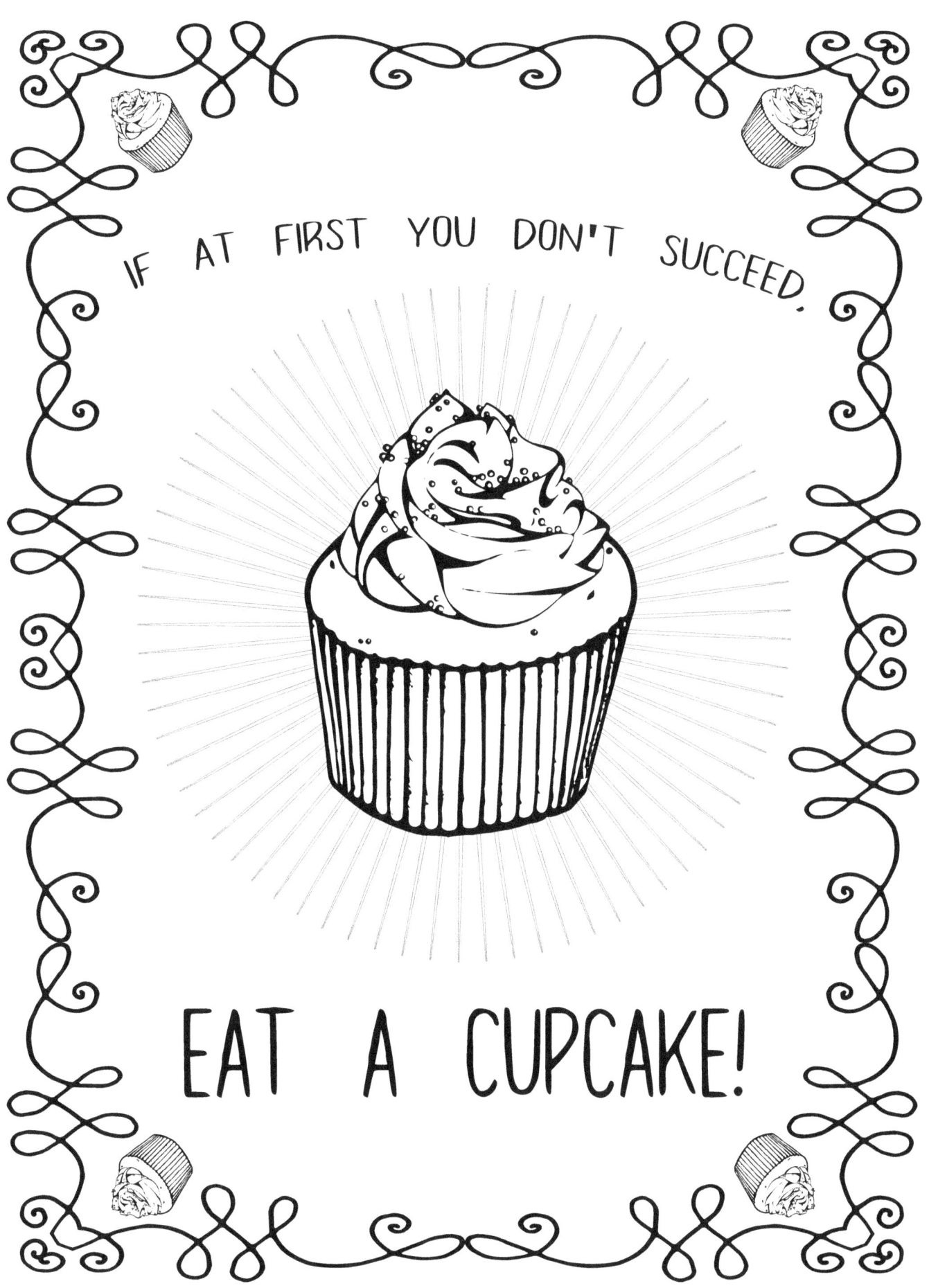

THERE ARE PEOPLE
IN THE WORLD
SO HUNGRY,
THAT GOD CANNOT
APPEAR TO THEM
EXCEPT
IN THE FORM
OF BREAD.
- MAHATMA GANDHI

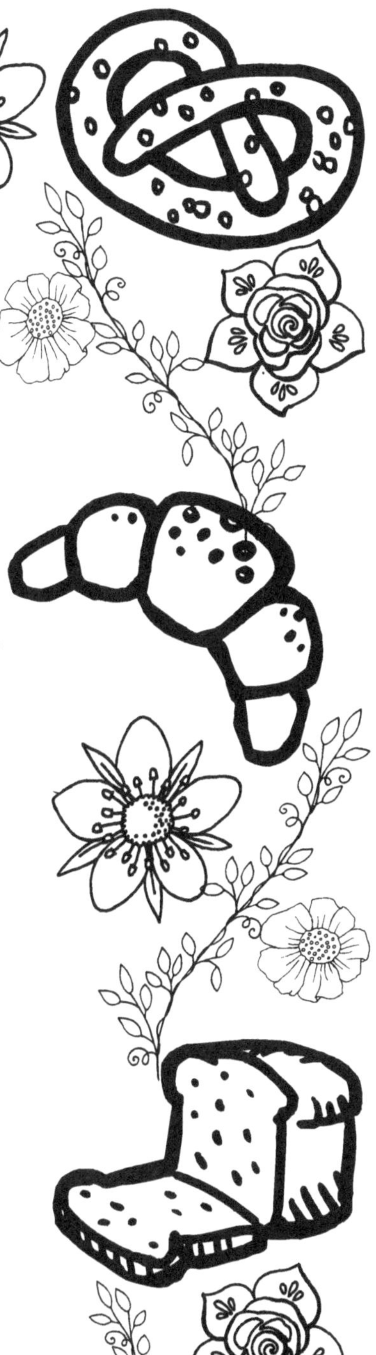

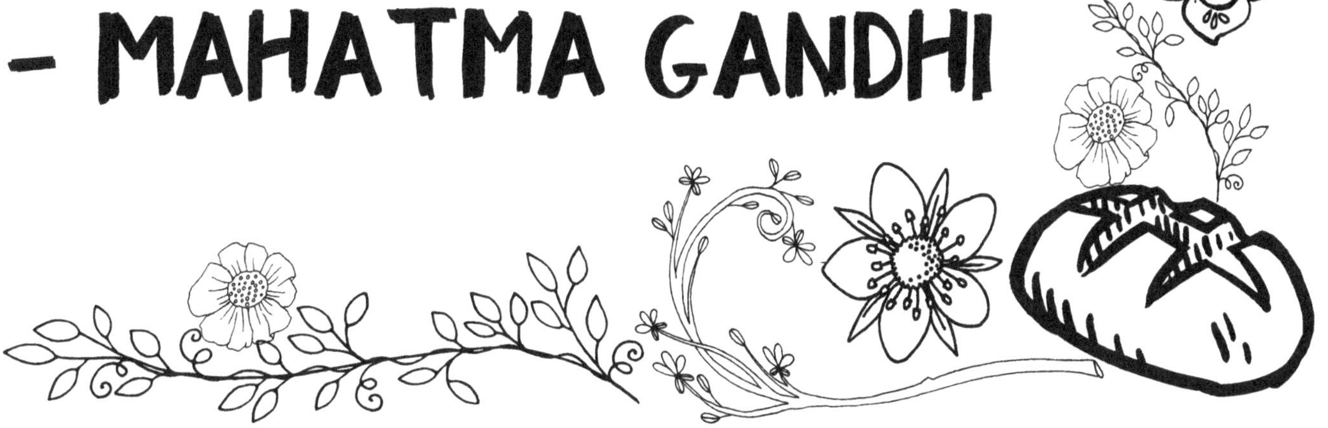

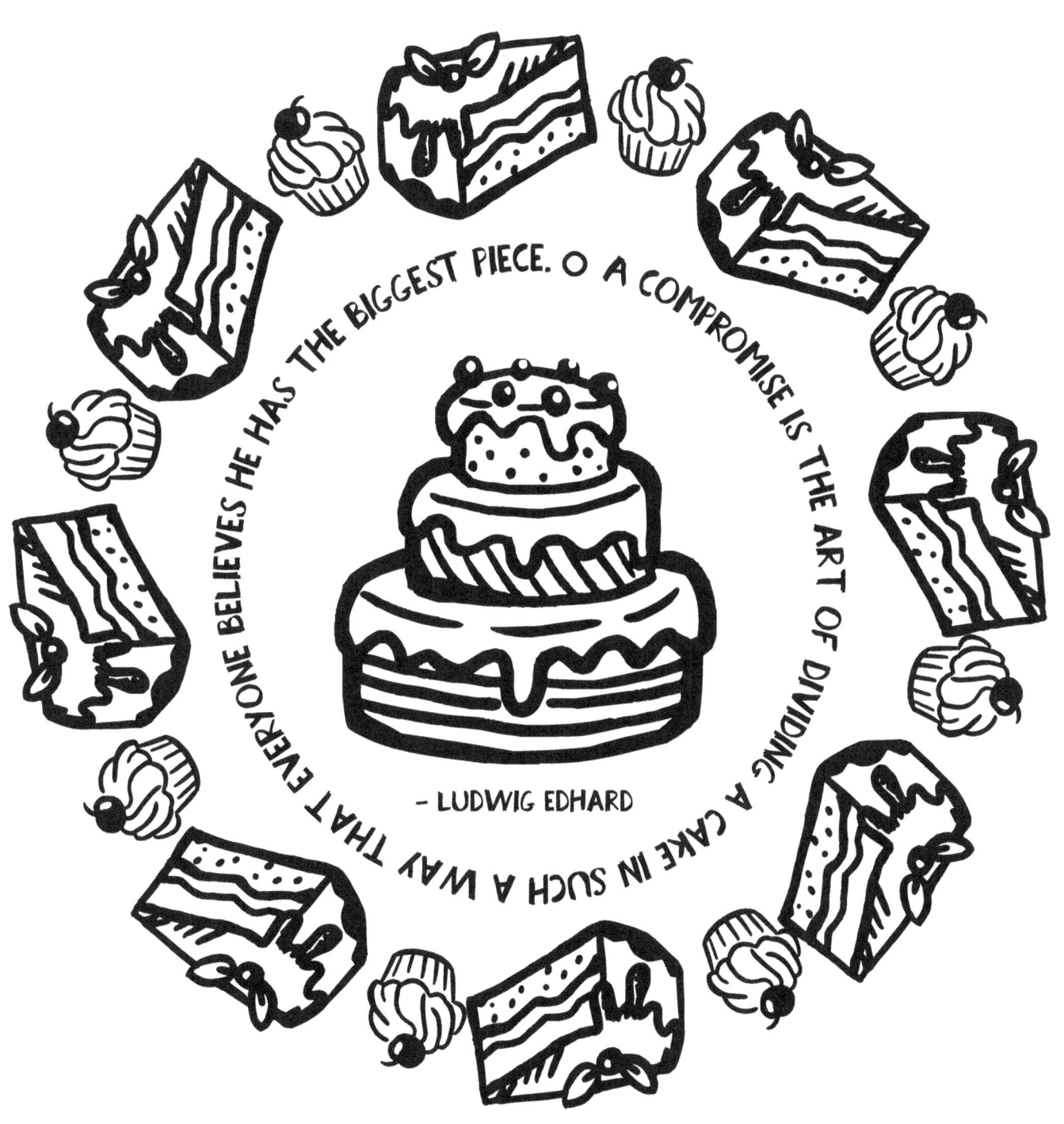

A COMPROMISE IS THE ART OF DIVIDING A CAKE IN SUCH A WAY THAT EVERYONE BELIEVES HE HAS THE BIGGEST PIECE.

– LUDWIG EDHARD

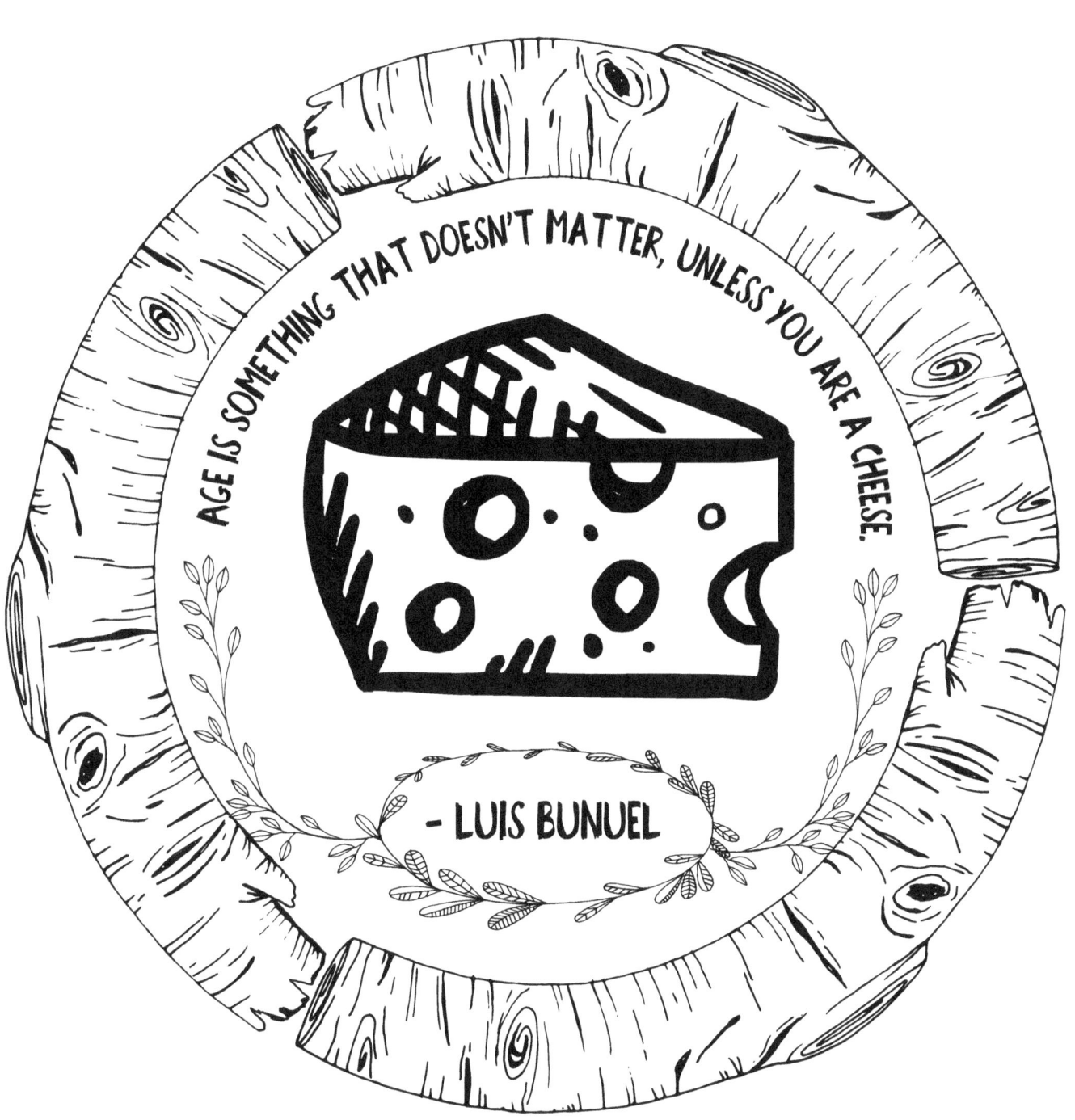

AGE IS SOMETHING THAT DOESN'T MATTER, UNLESS YOU ARE A CHEESE.

- LUIS BUNUEL

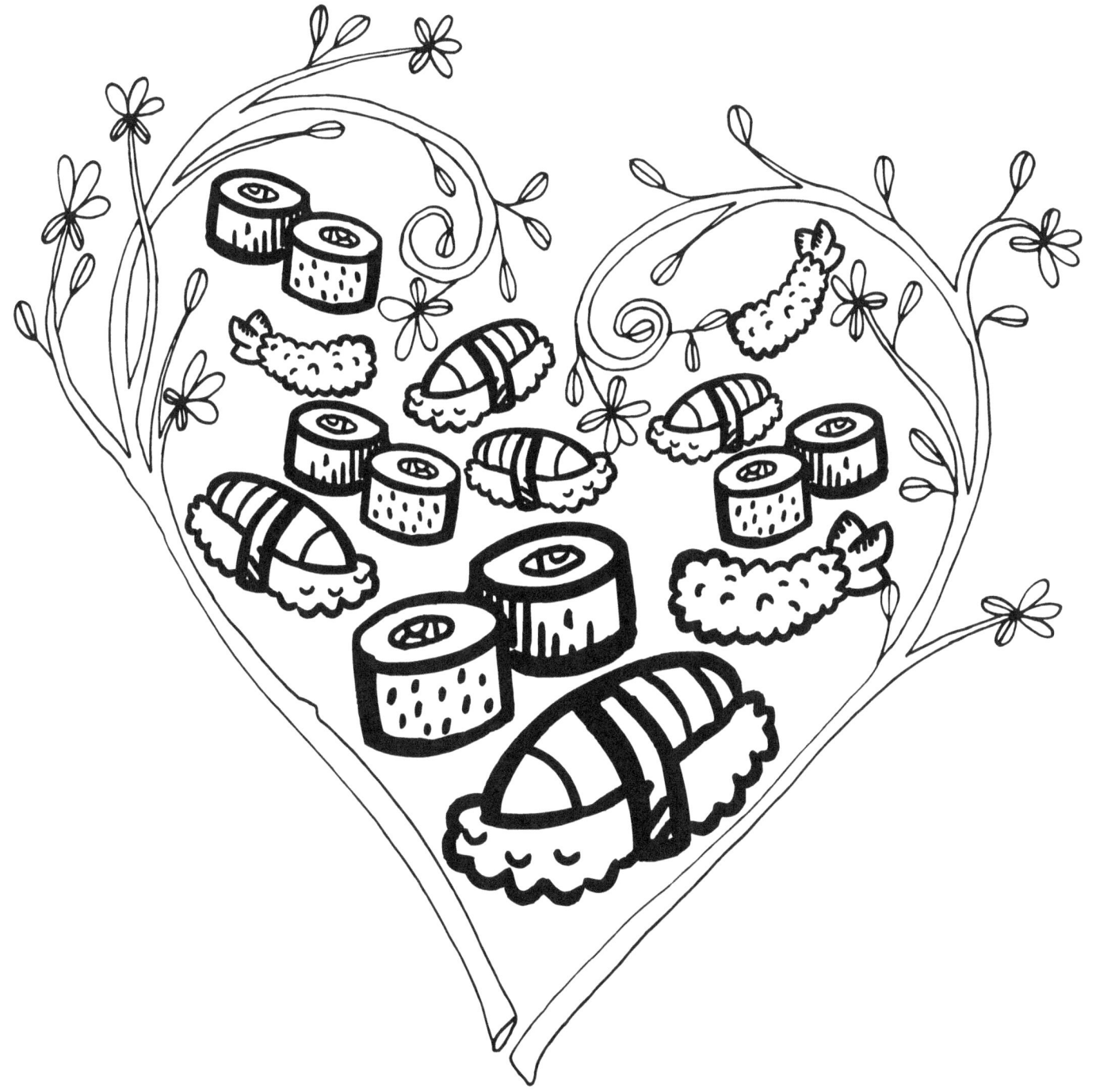

But you can't just

sit around

the fireplace

and sip Cokes

and eat pretzels

and get

an attitude of confidence.

You have to put in hard work.

- Lee Haney

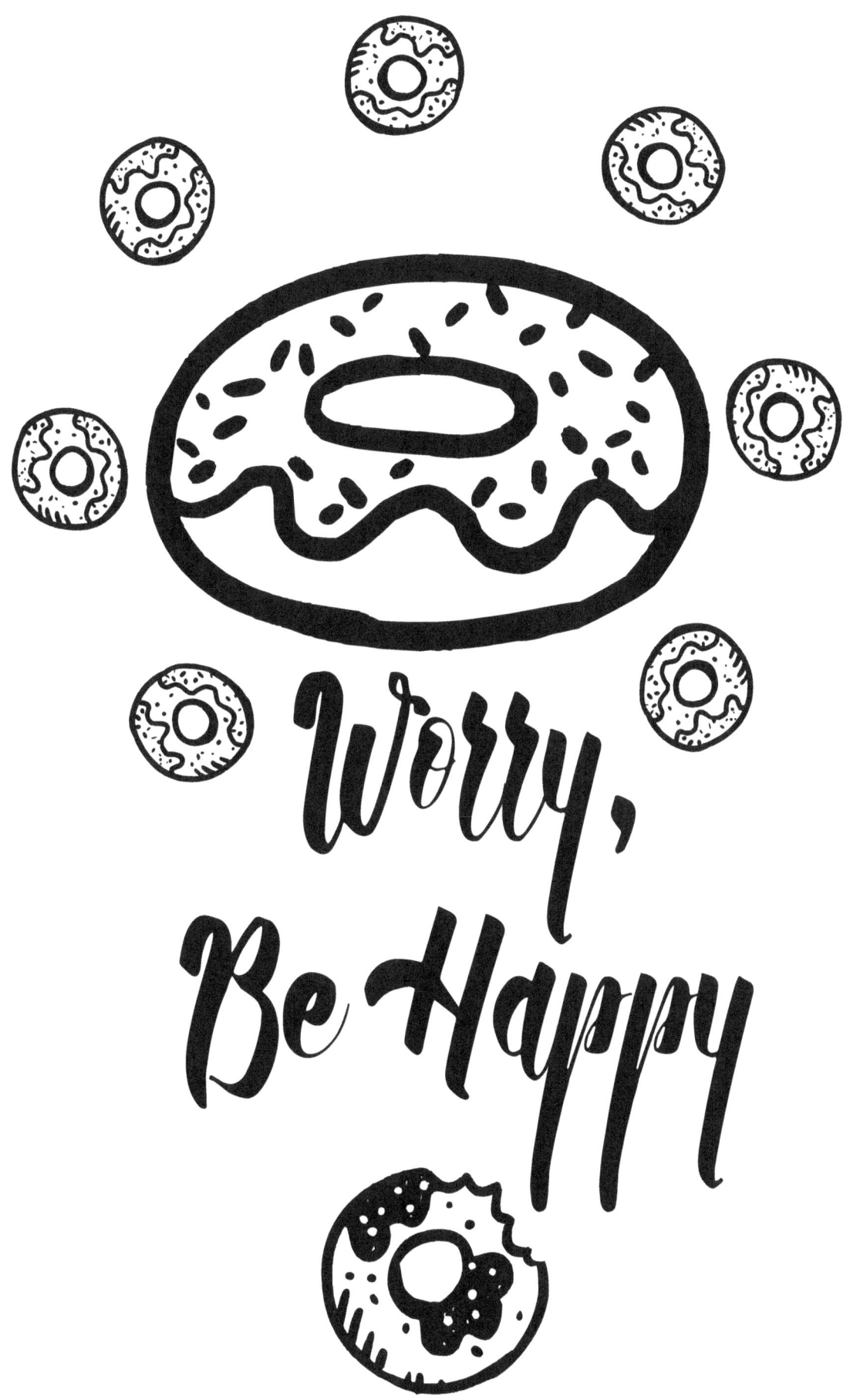

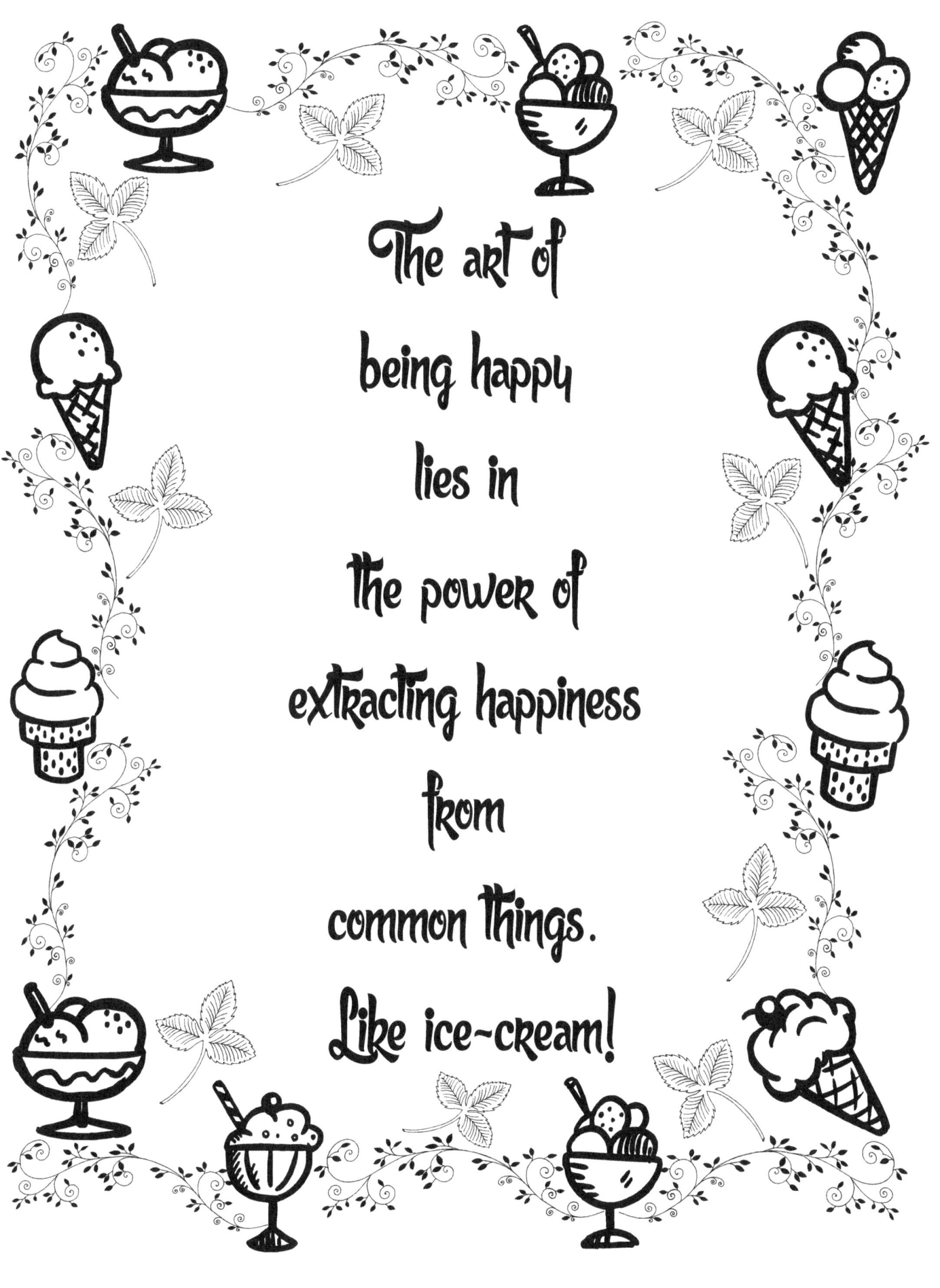

The art of
being happy
lies in
the power of
extracting happiness
from
common things.
Like ice-cream!

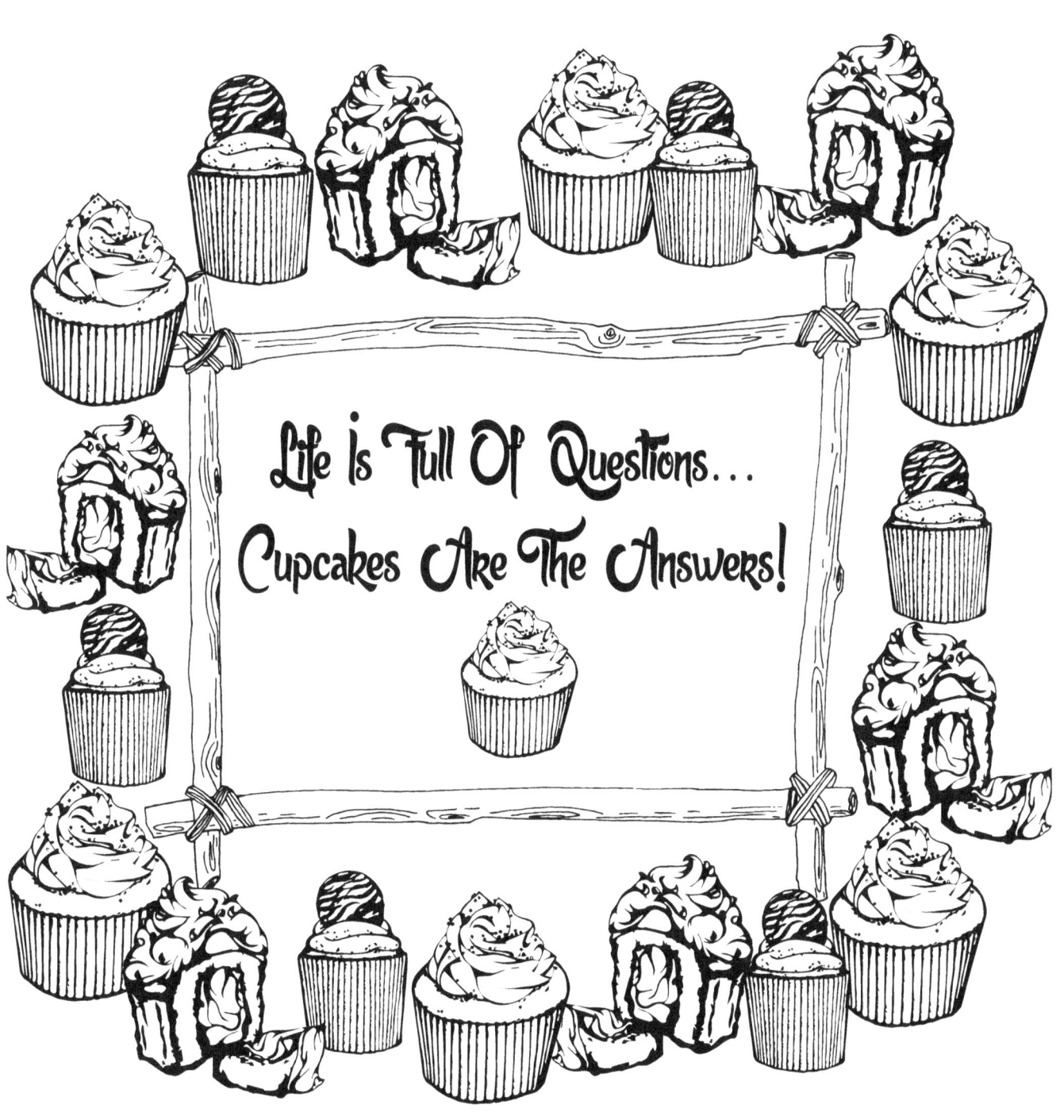

Life Is Full Of Questions...
Cupcakes Are The Answers!

Life Is A Combination

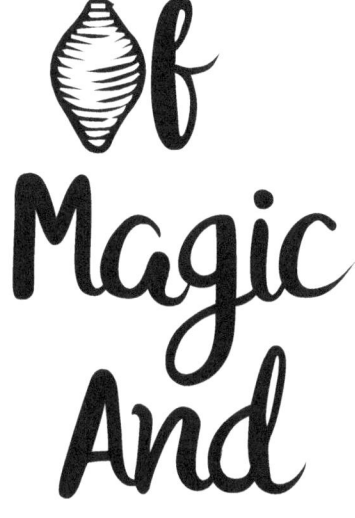

Of
Magic
And

Pasta!
- Federico Fellini

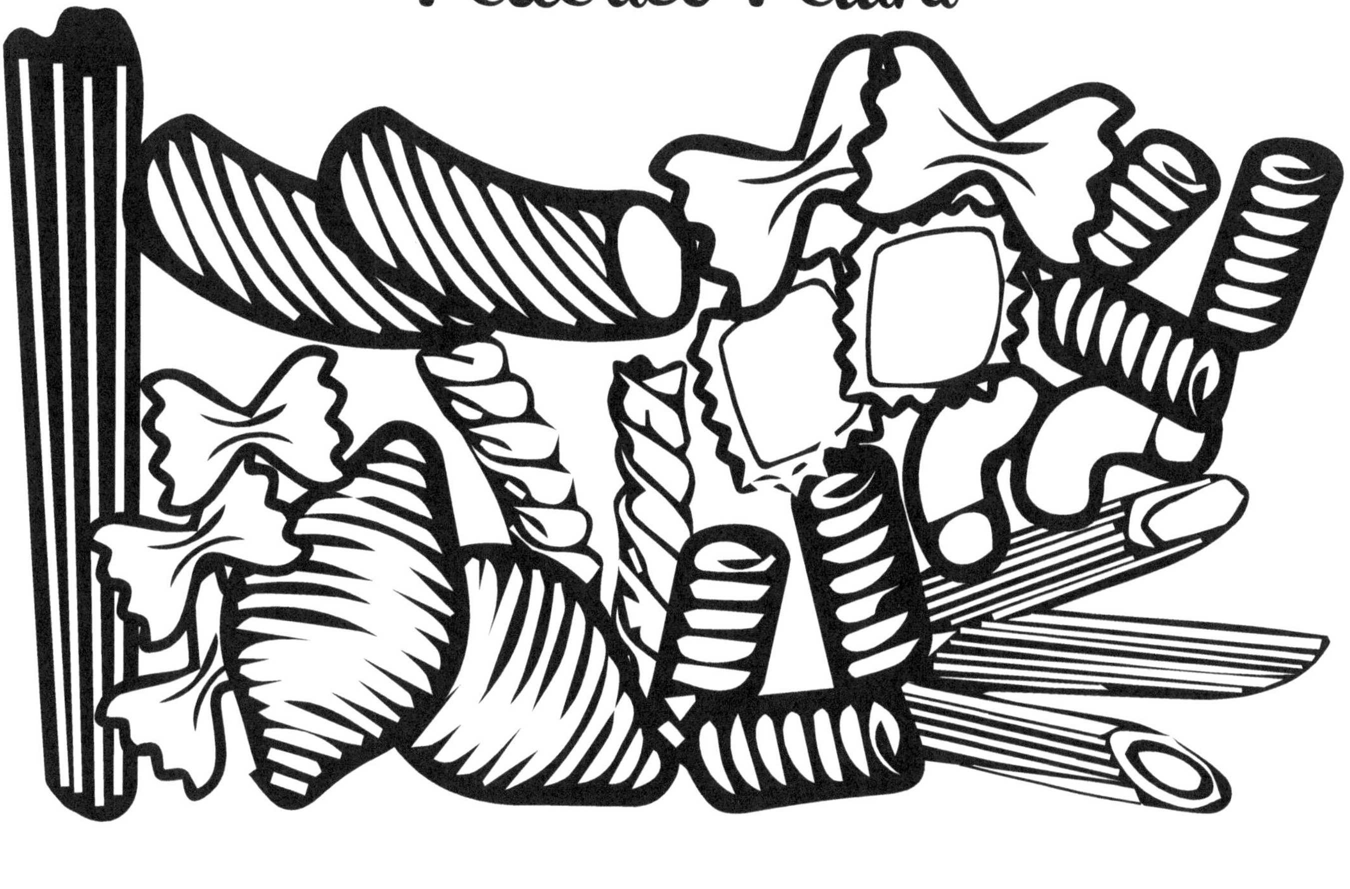

If You Hang Out With
Chickens,
You Are Going To Cluck
And If You Hang Out With
Eagles,
You Are Going To Fly.
– Steve Maraboli

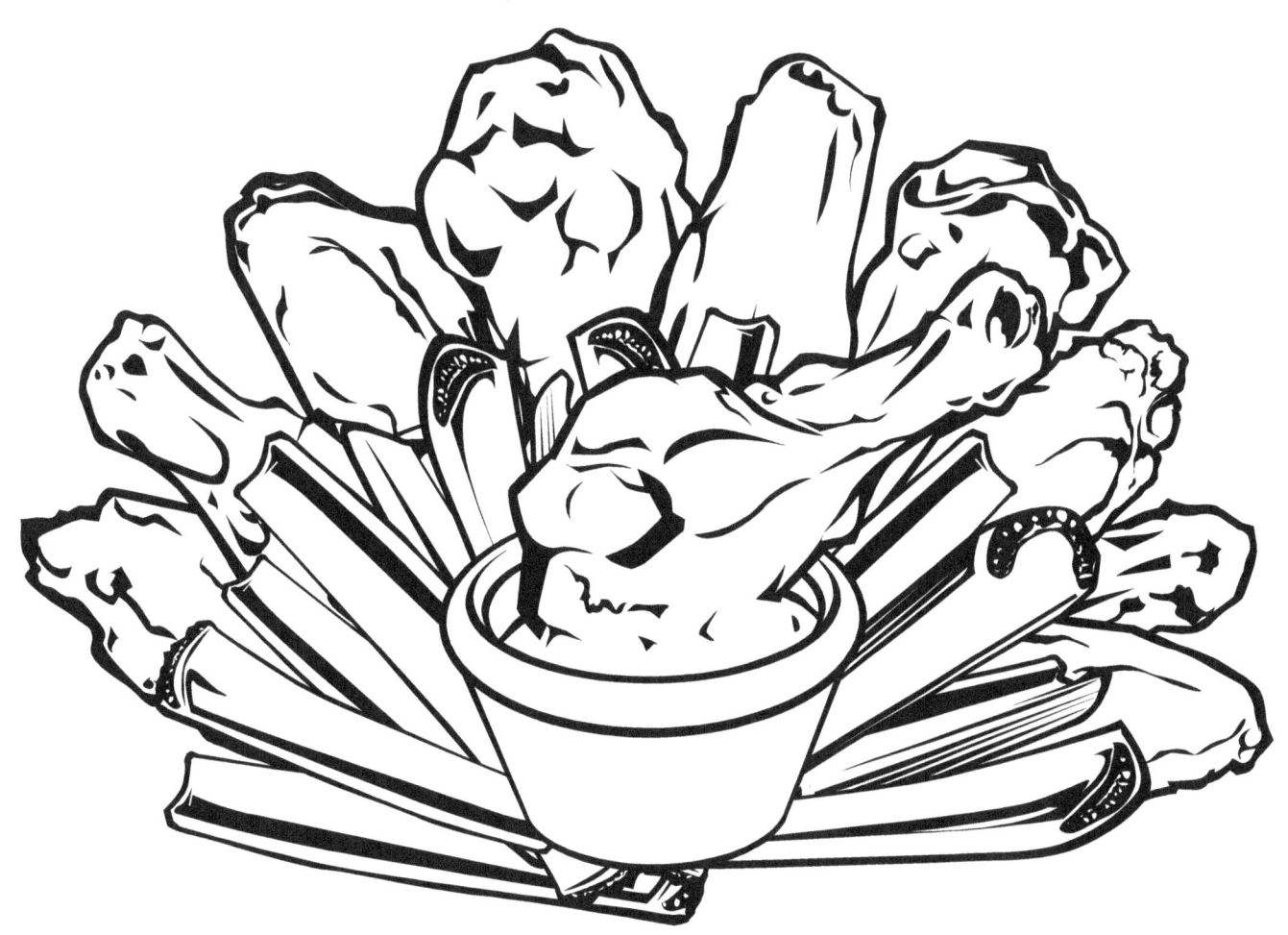

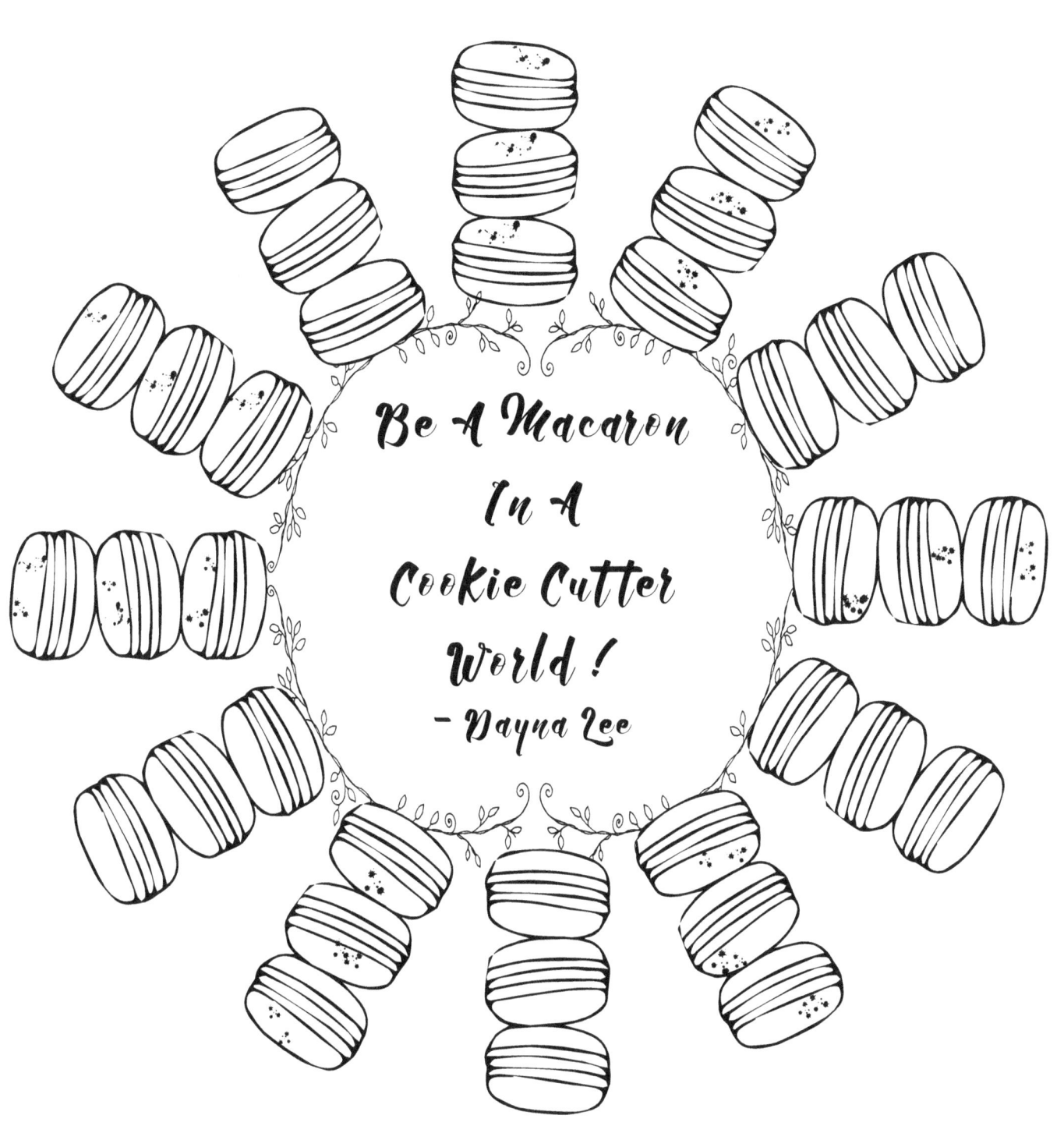

Be A Macaron
In A
Cookie Cutter
World !
- Dayna Lee

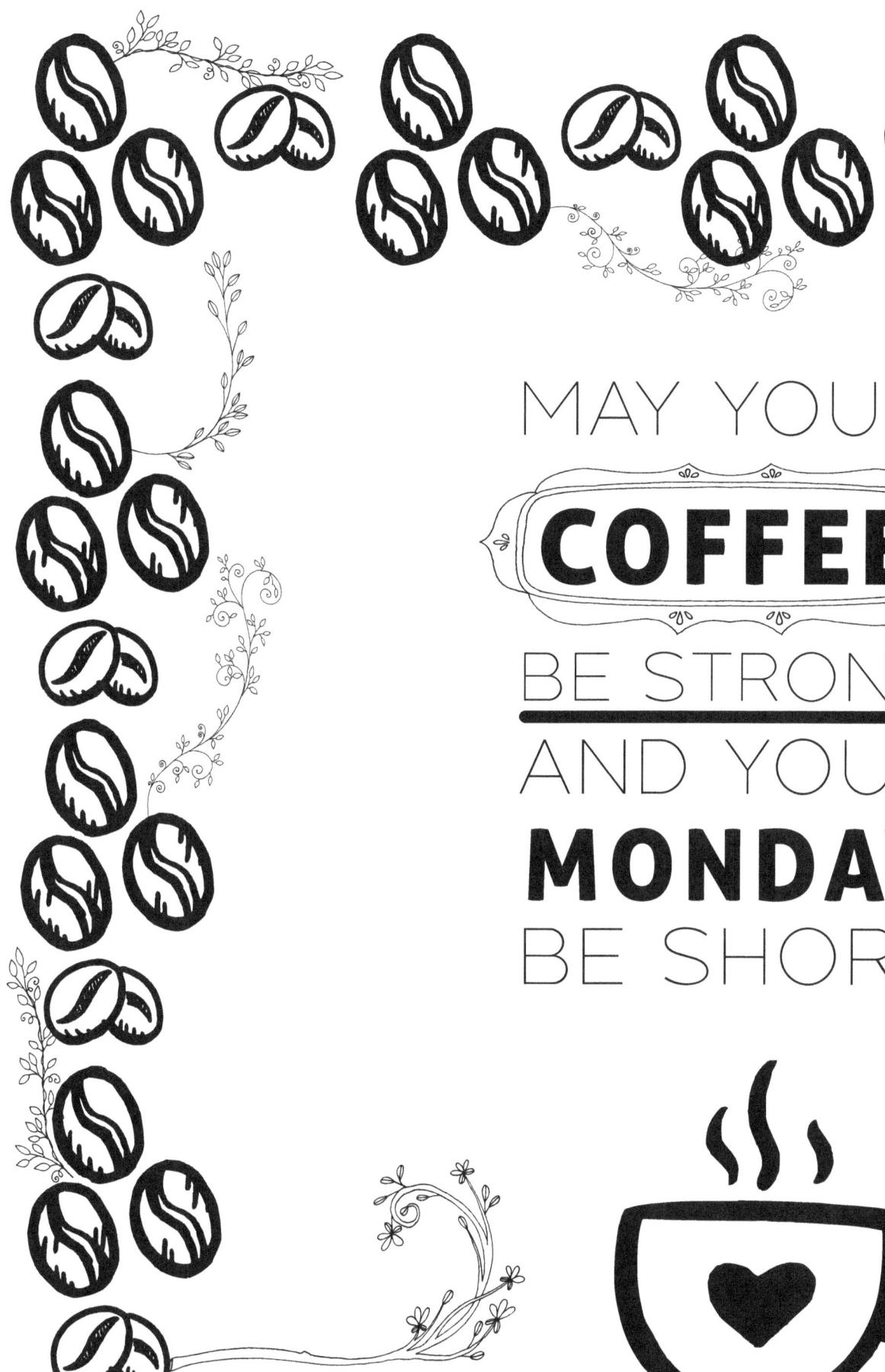

MAY YOUR

COFFEE

BE STRONG

AND YOUR

MONDAY

BE SHORT

I DON'T LIKE TO DISCUSS
MY MARRIAGE,
BUT I WILL TELL YOU
SOMETHING WHICH MAY
SOUND CORNY BUT
WHICH HAPPENS TO
BE TRUE.

I HAVE STEAK AT HOME,

WHY SHOULD I GO OUT
AND GET A HAMBURGER?

- PAUL NEWMAN

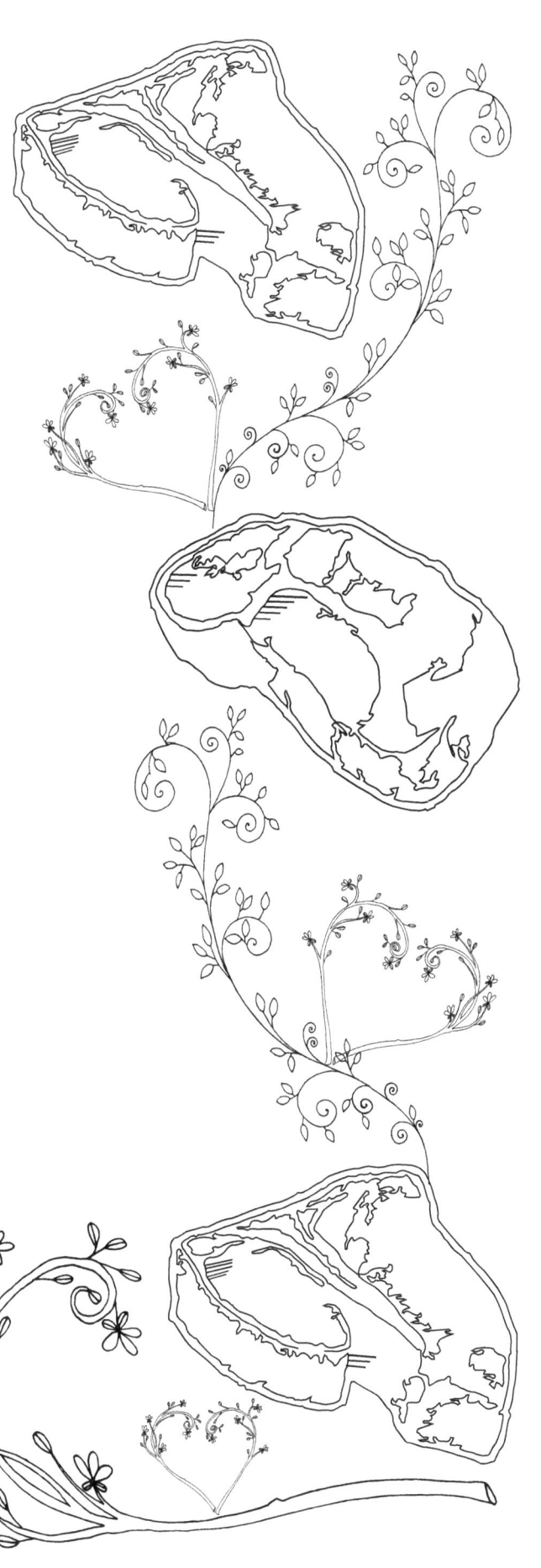

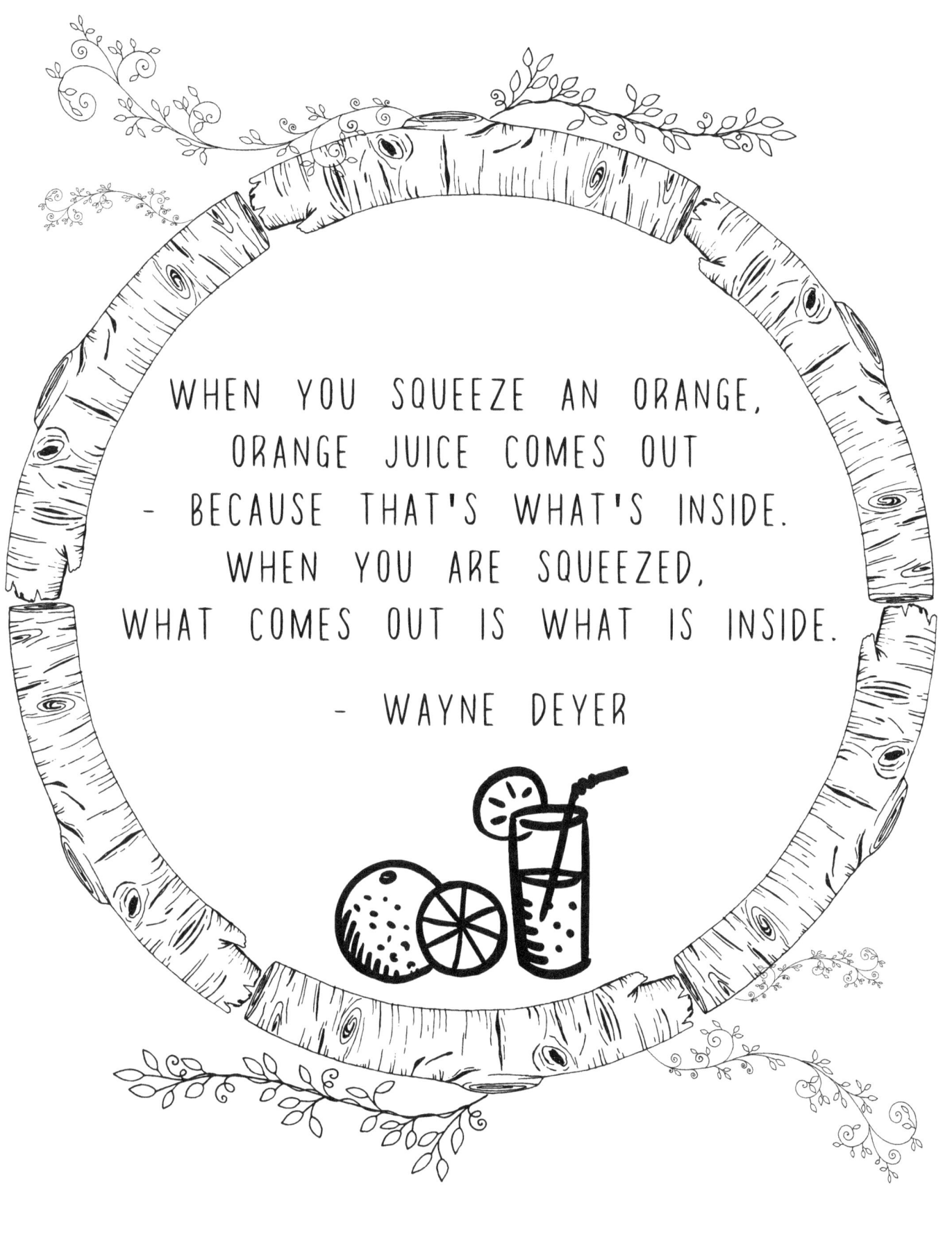

WHEN YOU SQUEEZE AN ORANGE,
ORANGE JUICE COMES OUT
- BECAUSE THAT'S WHAT'S INSIDE.
WHEN YOU ARE SQUEEZED,
WHAT COMES OUT IS WHAT IS INSIDE.

- WAYNE DEYER

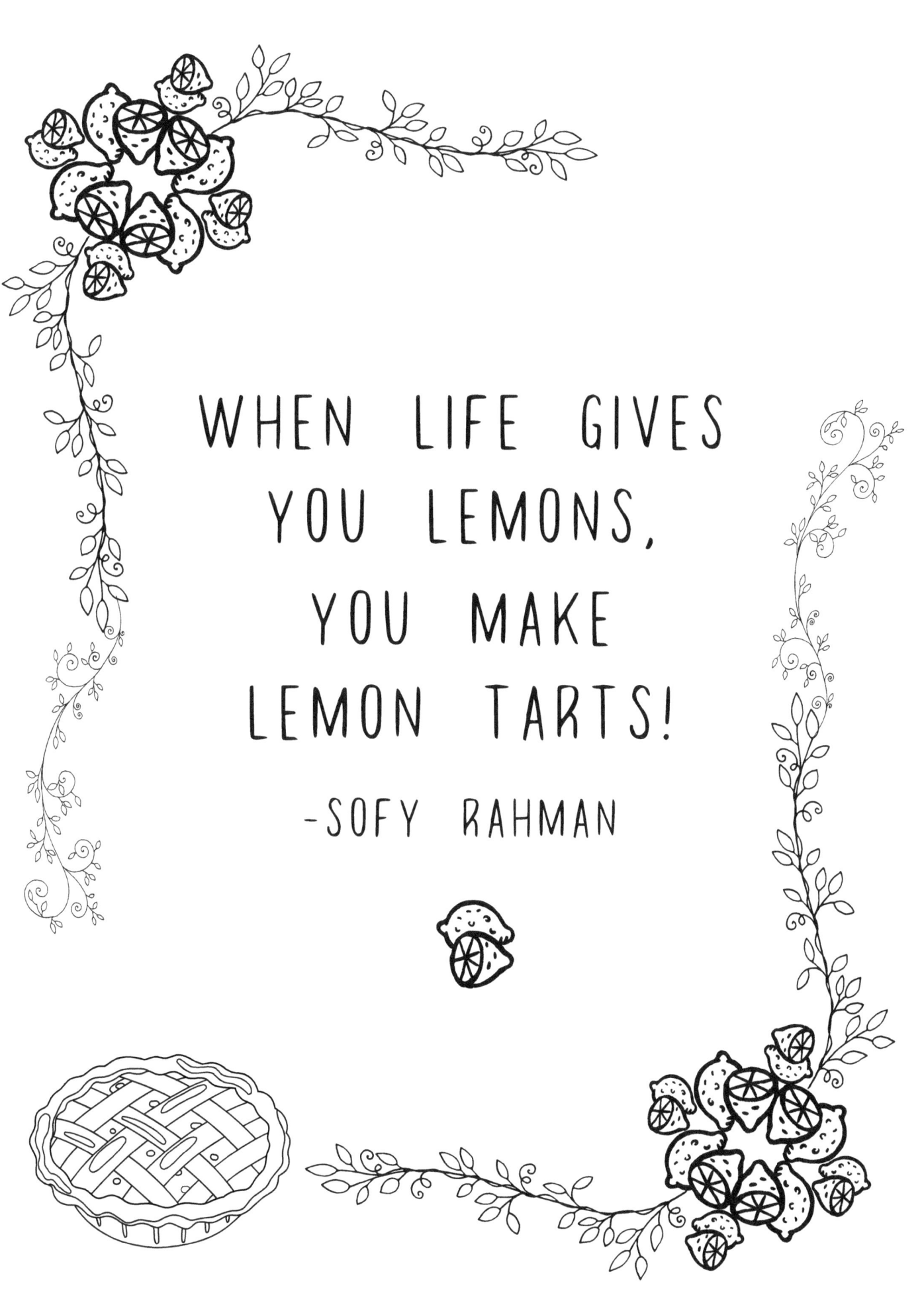

WHEN LIFE GIVES
YOU LEMONS,
YOU MAKE
LEMON TARTS!

-SOFY RAHMAN

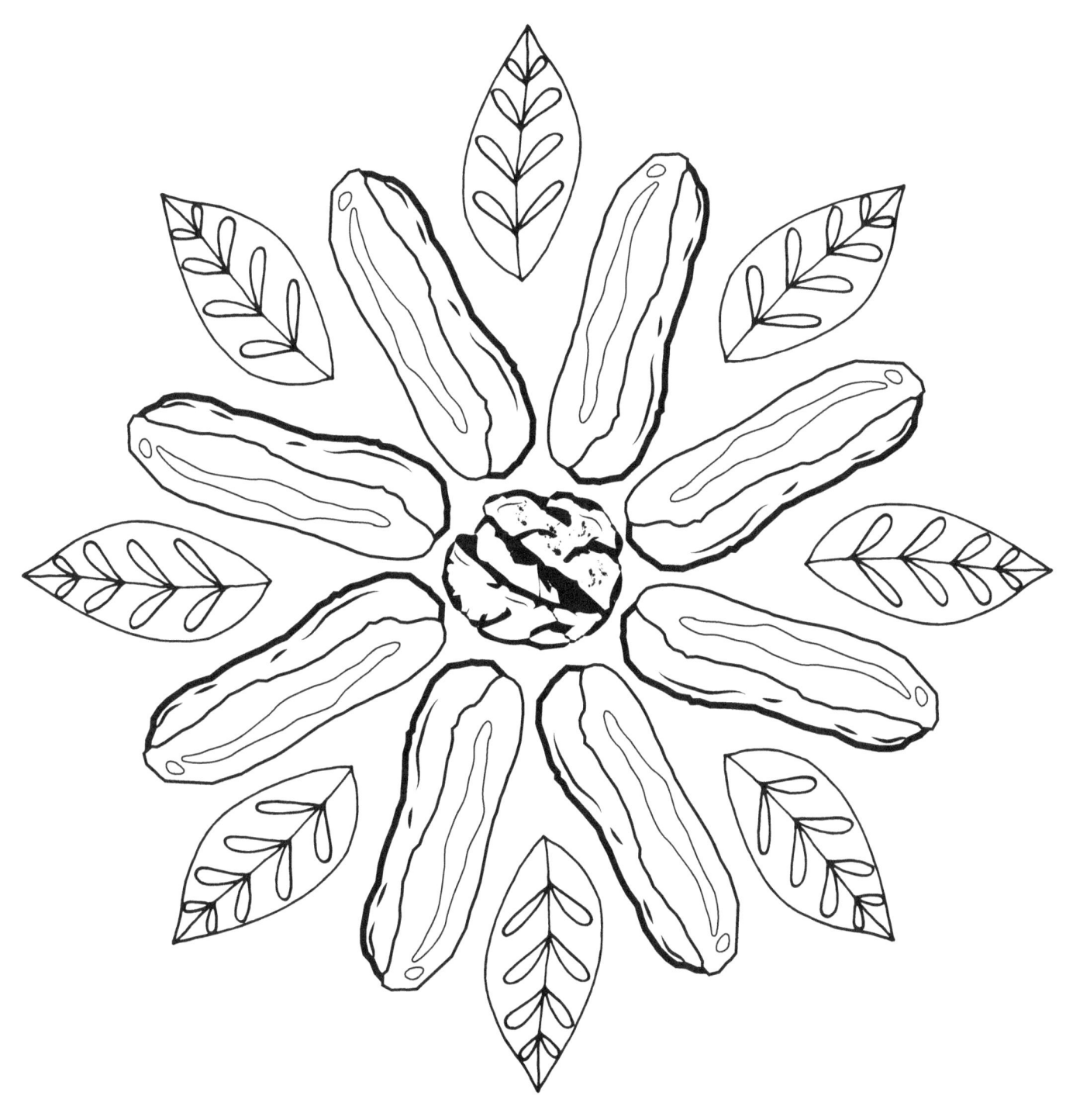

We Become What We Think About.
I Am An Eclair.

- Earl Nightingale

FLIPPING BURGERS IS **NOT BENEATH** YOUR Dignity. YOUR GRANPARENTS HAD A **DIFFERENT** WORD FOR  FLIPPING. Opportunity.

- Bill Gates

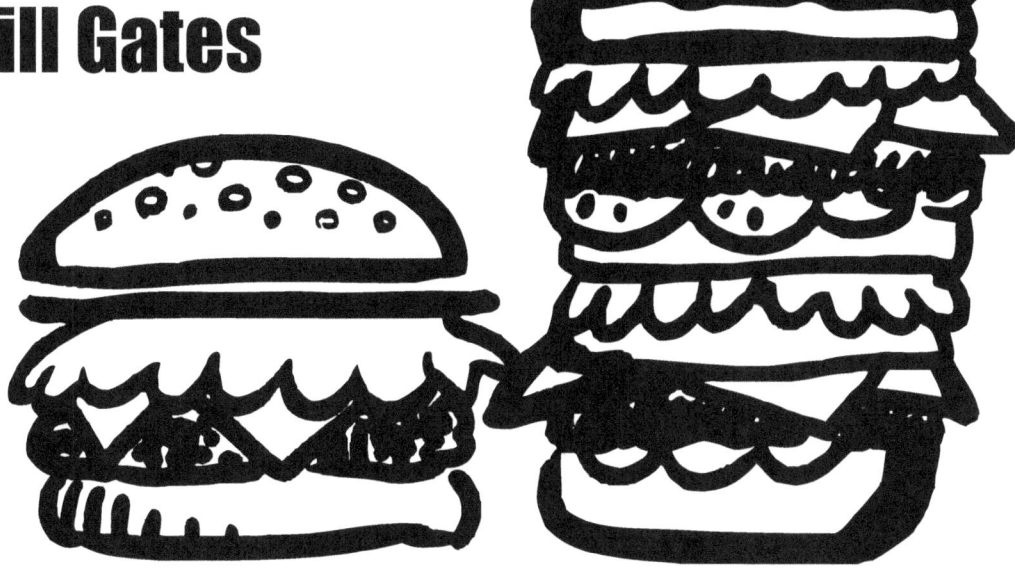

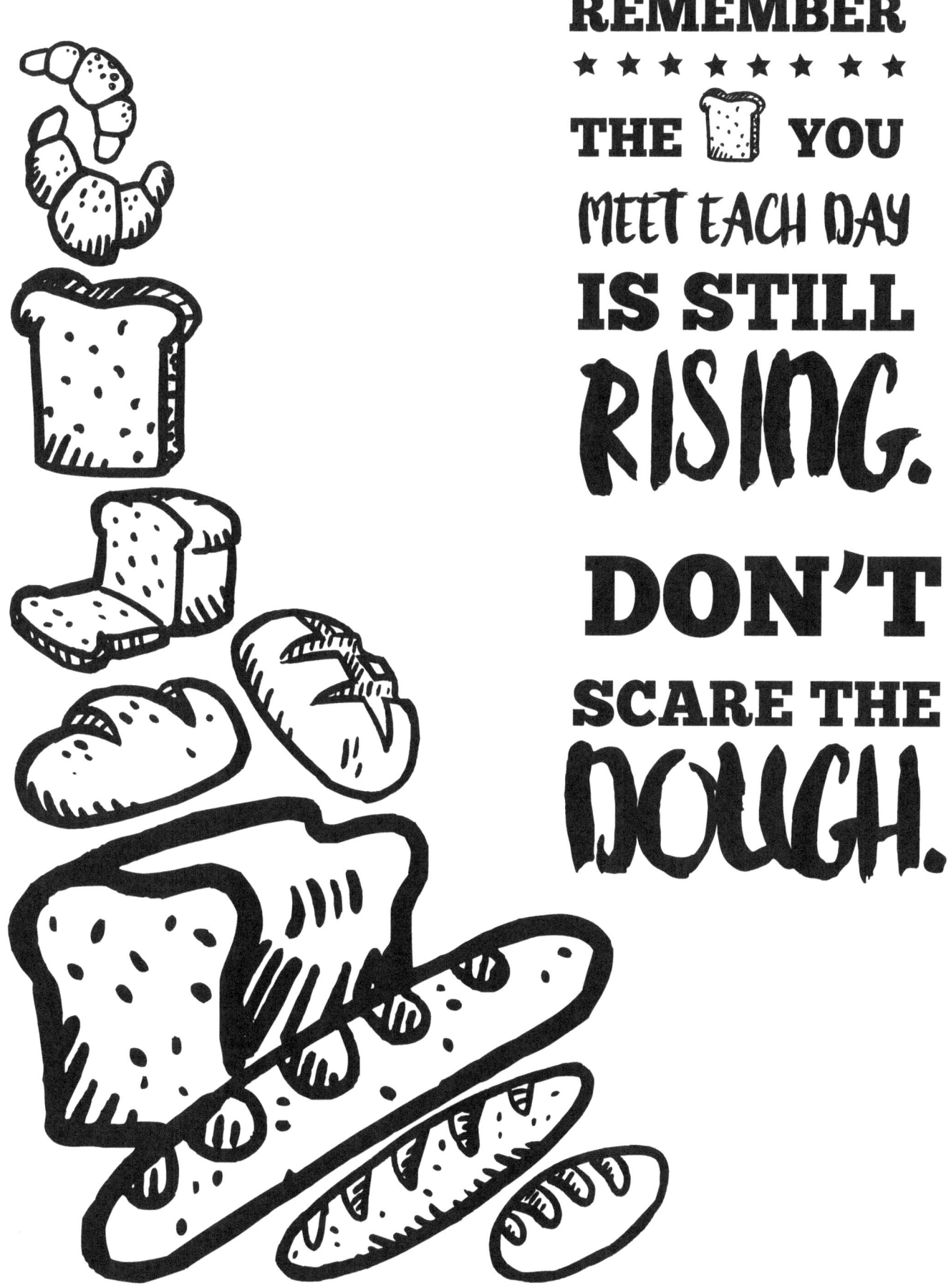

REMEMBER
★ ★ ★ ★ ★ ★ ★ ★
THE 🍞 YOU MEET EACH DAY IS STILL RISING. DON'T SCARE THE DOUGH.

Love is like a good cake;
you never know
when it's coming,

but you'd better eat it
when it does!

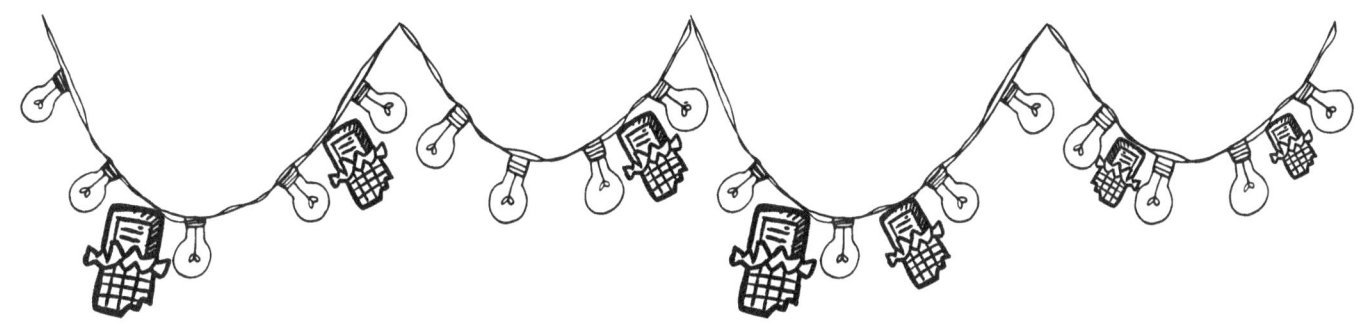

Strength...

is the ABILITY

to break a 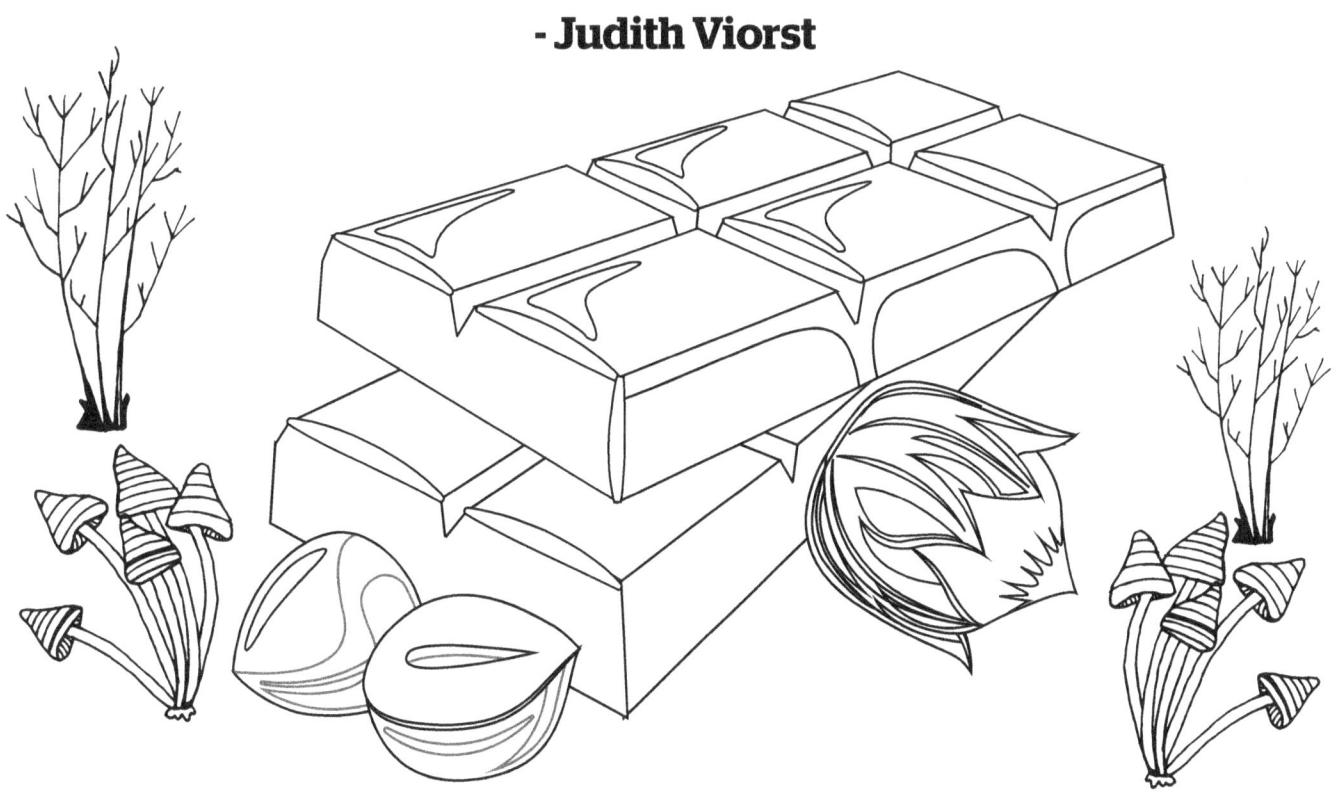 bar

into 4 pieces

with your bare hands

- and then EAT just one of those pieces!

- Judith Viorst

EAT
HUMBLE PIE.

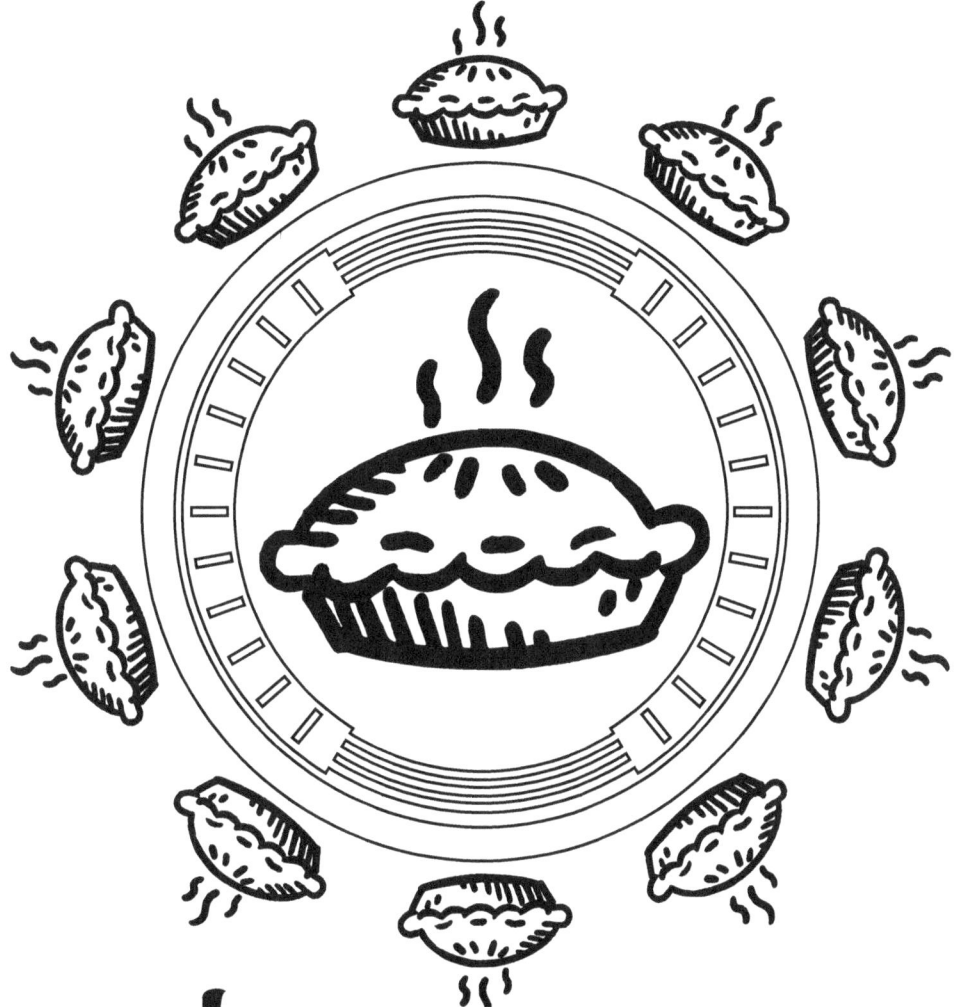

If YOU MAKE
A ~~MISTAKE~~, ADMIT it.

IF SOMEONE BREAKS YOUR 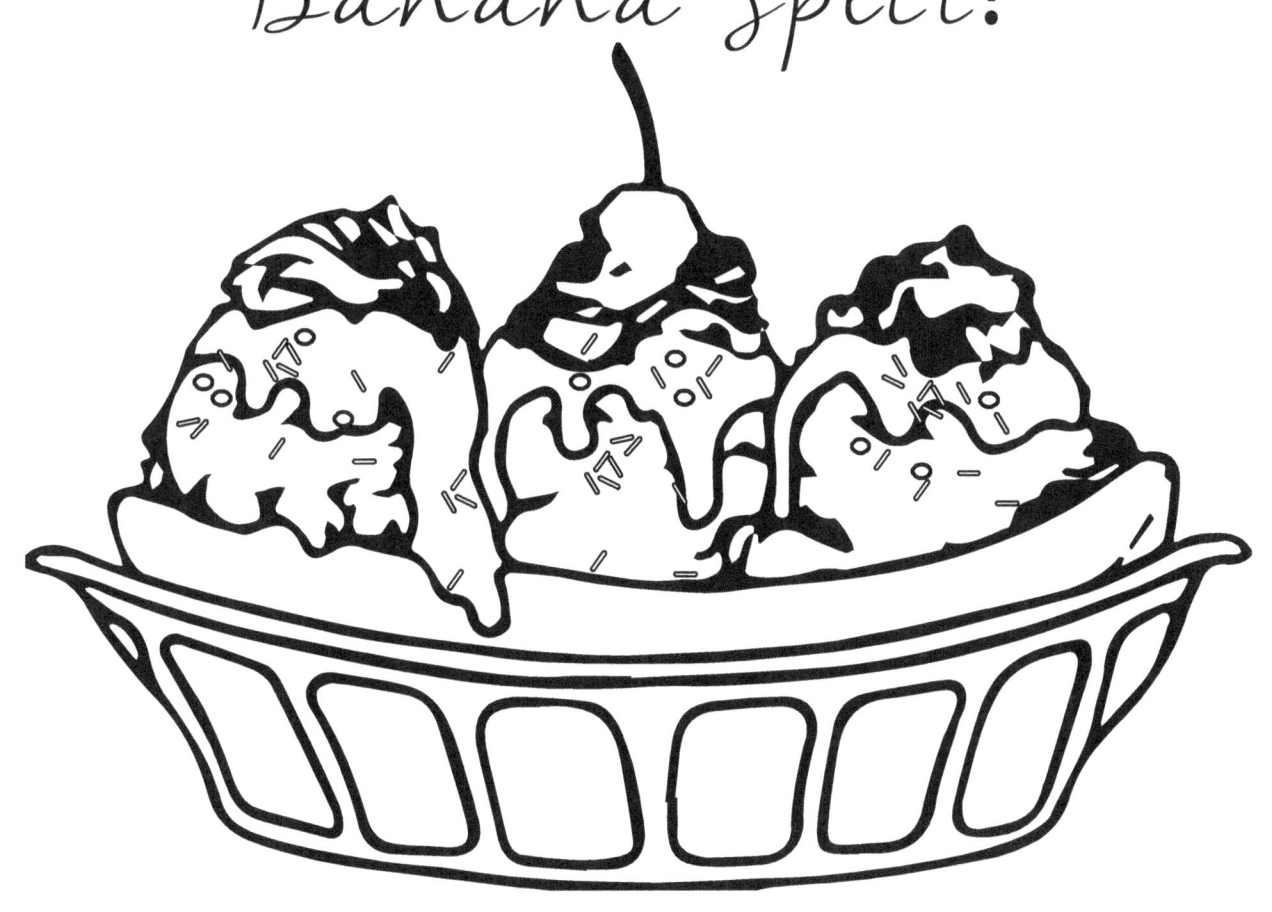,
JUST PUNCH THEM
IN THE FACE.
Seriously.
PUNCH THEM IN THE
FACE AND GO GET A
Banana Split!

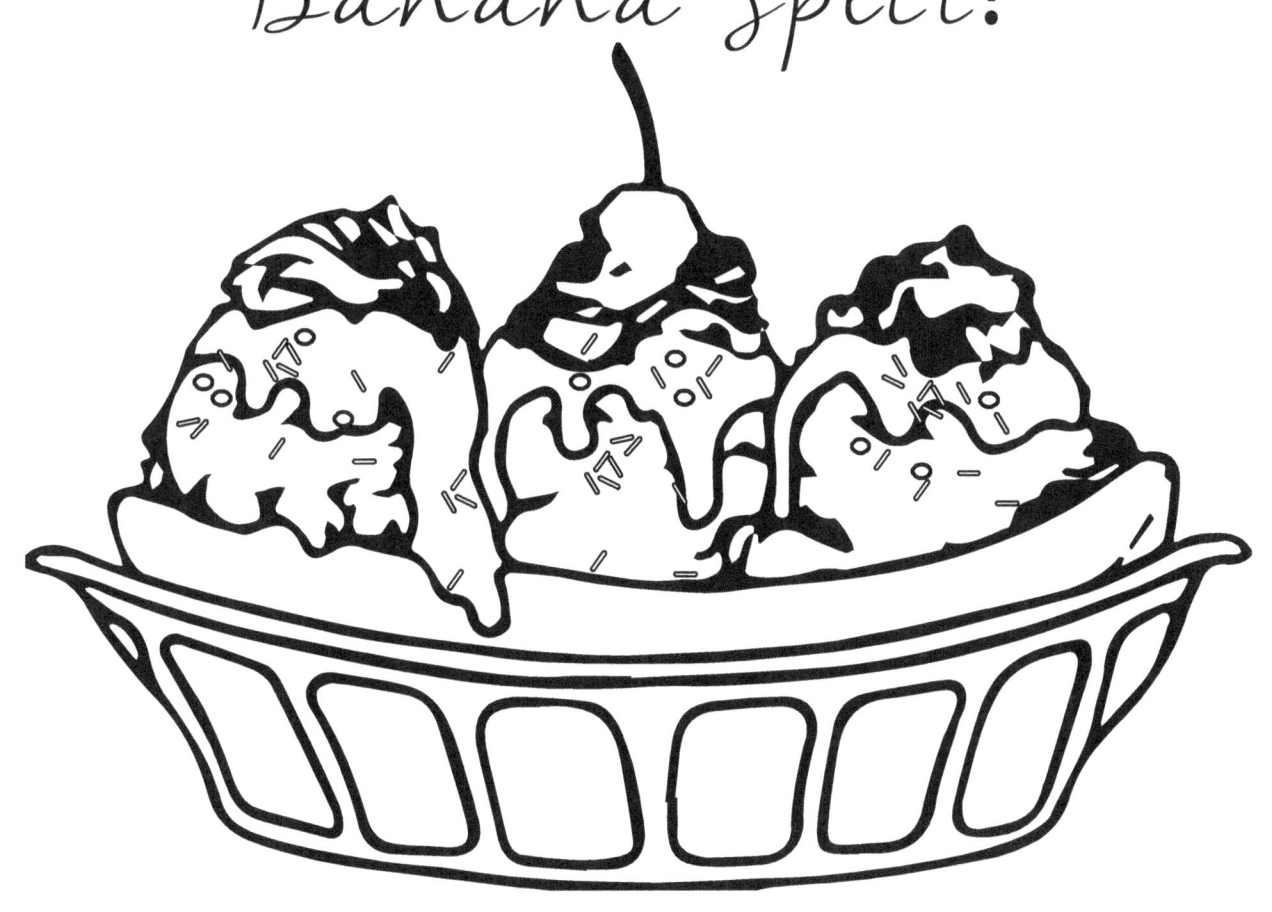

ANYONE WHO GIVES YOU A CINNAMON ROLL FRESH OUT OF THE OVEN IS A FRIEND for life!

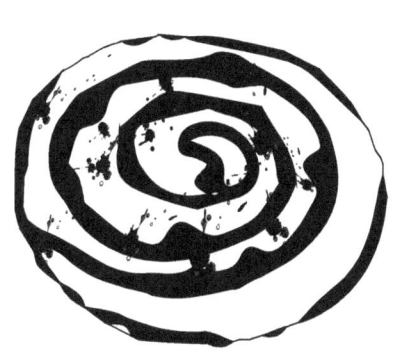

WHEN YOU

ARE FEELING

DOWN-Y,

GRAB YOURSELF

SOME BROWNIE!

- SOFY RAHMAN

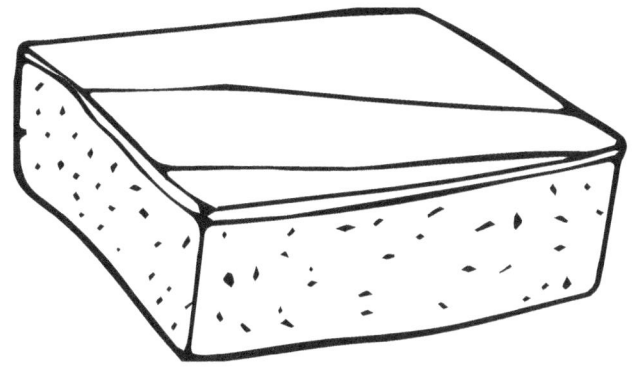

TRY NOT TO
BE LIKE

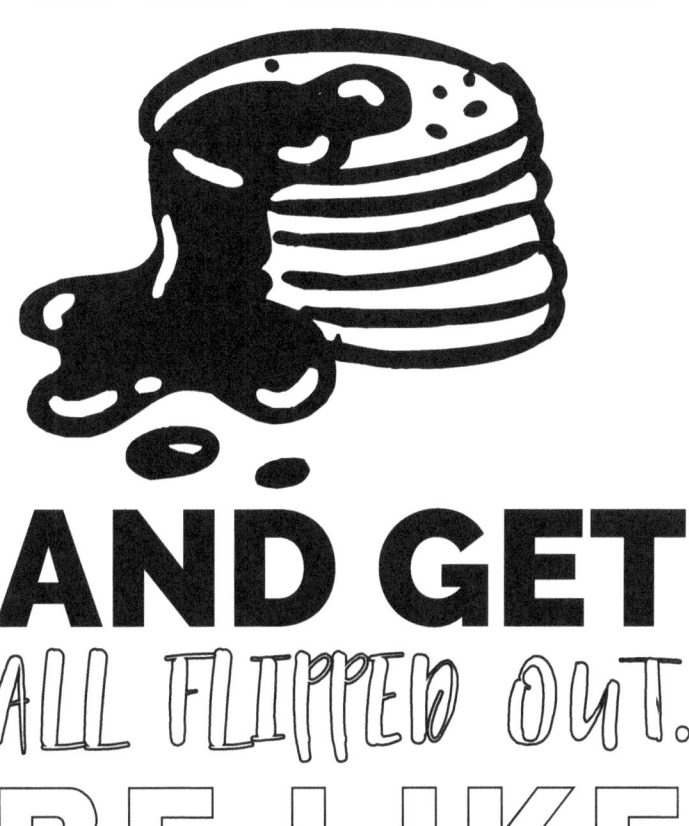

AND GET
ALL FLIPPED OUT.
BE LIKE
SYRUP
AND GO
WITH THE FLOW!

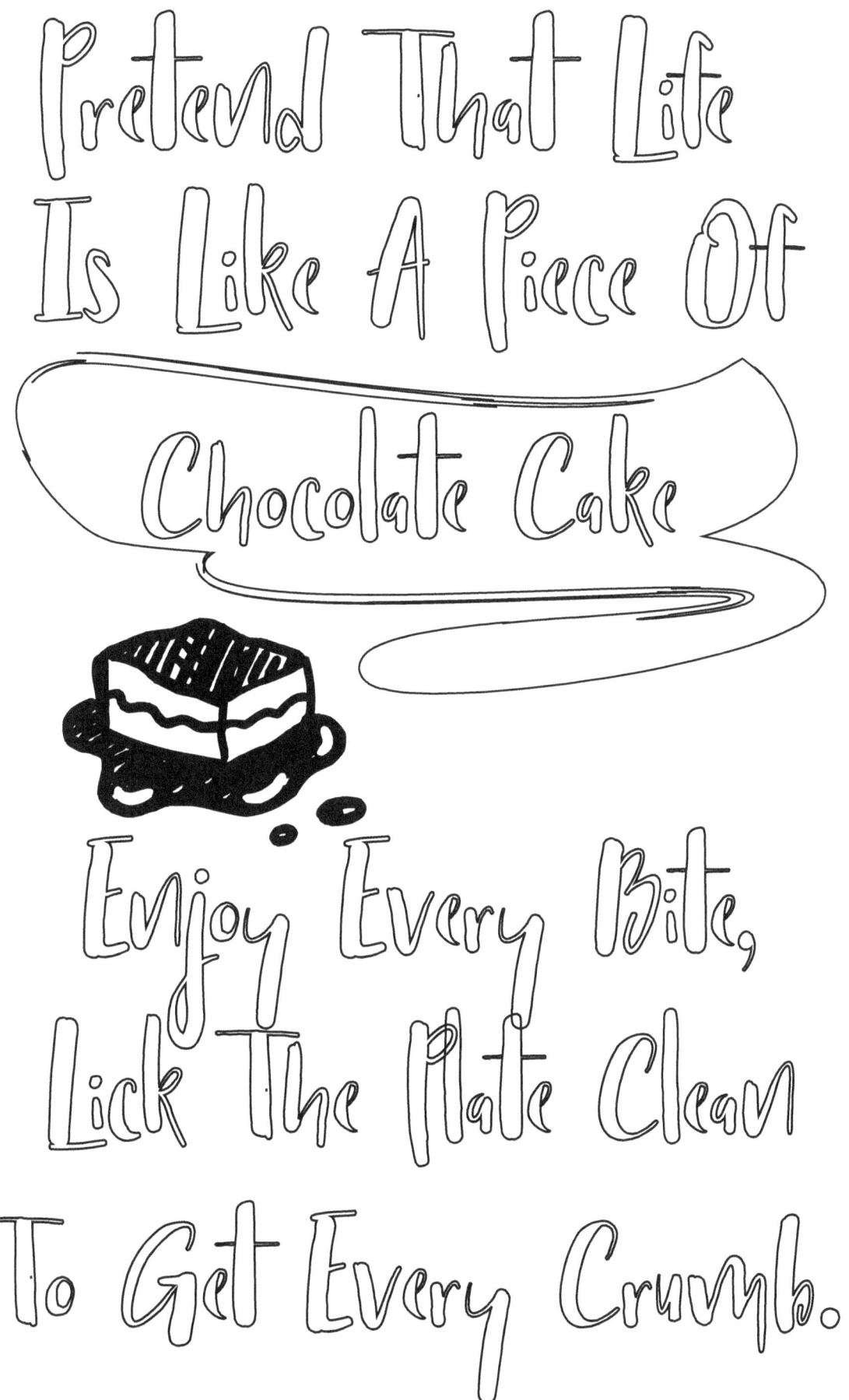

Pretend That Life
Is Like A Piece Of

Chocolate Cake

Enjoy Every Bite,
Lick The Plate Clean
To Get Every Crumb.

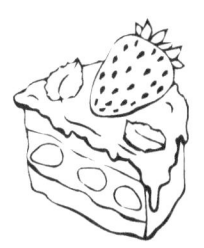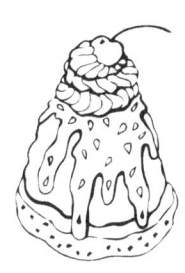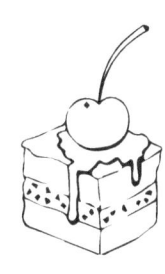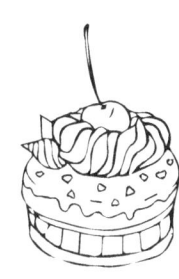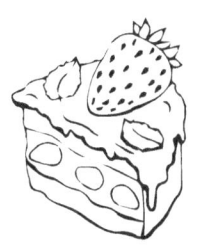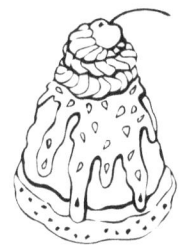

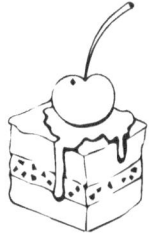
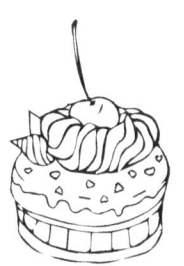

LIFE IS ABOUT *falling in* ♥ WITH THE *right* PERSON, *shopping,* EATING YOUR FAVOURITE *desserts* AND *travelling* A LOT.

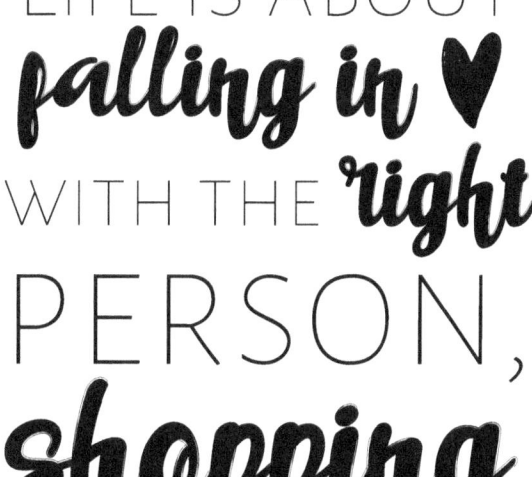
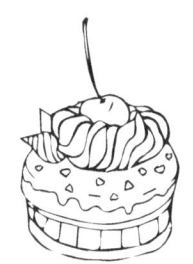
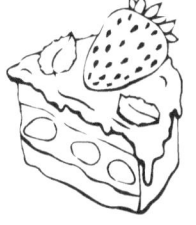
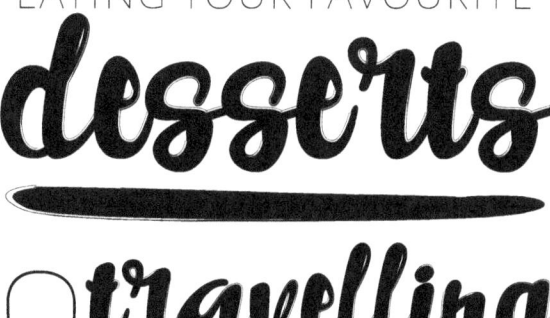
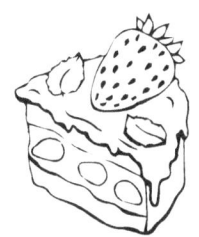
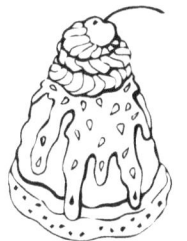
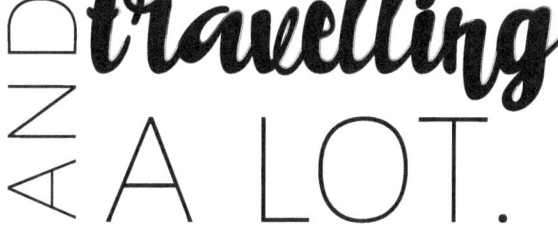
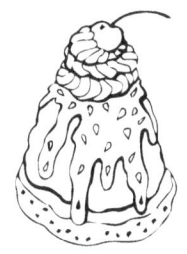

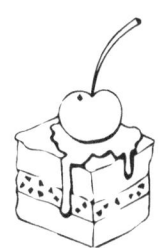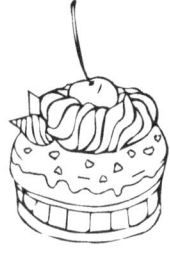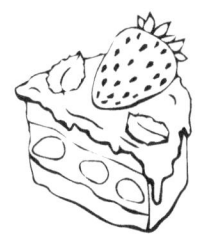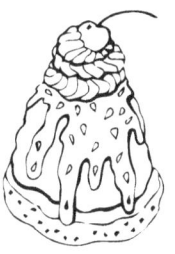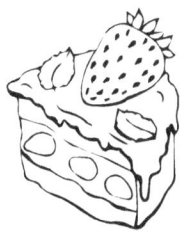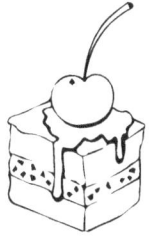

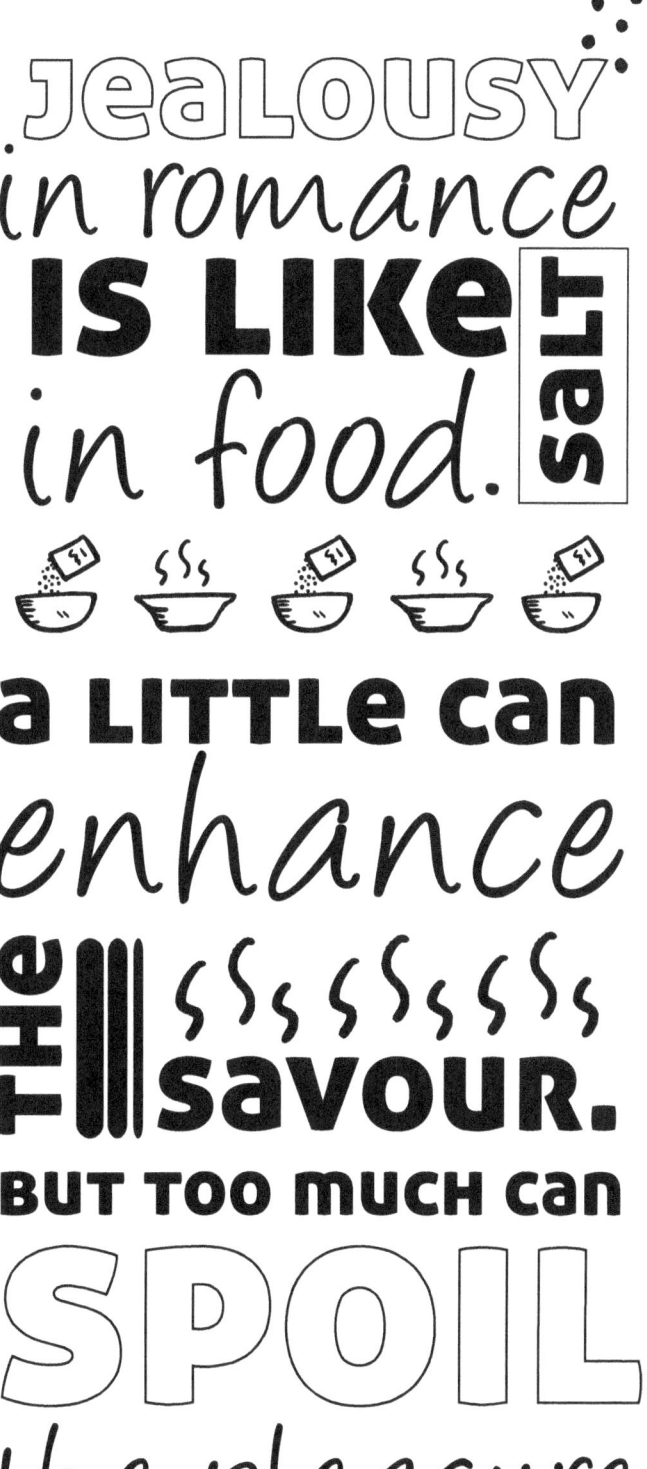

Jealousy in romance IS LIKE salt in food.

a LITTLE can enhance THE savour.

BUT TOO MUCH CAN SPOIL the pleasure.

 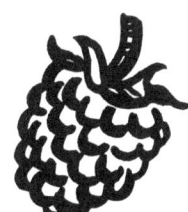 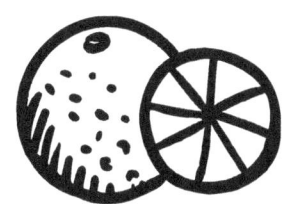 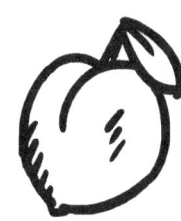 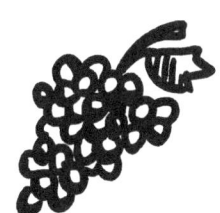

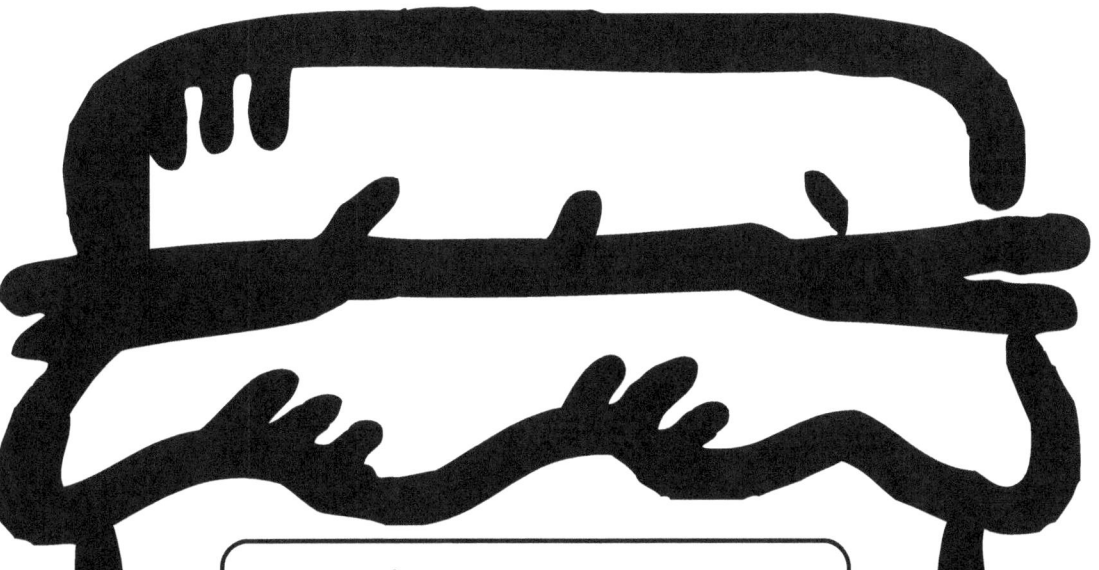

Happiness

IS LIKE JAM

You Can't Spread

EVEN A LITTLE

Without Getting

SOME ON YOURSELF!

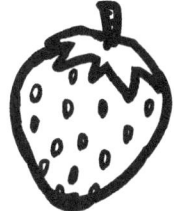 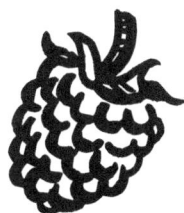 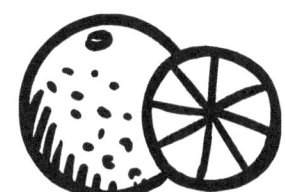 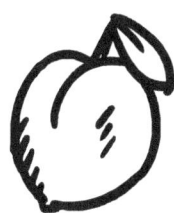 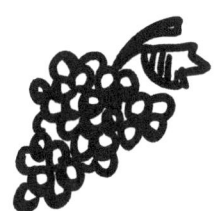

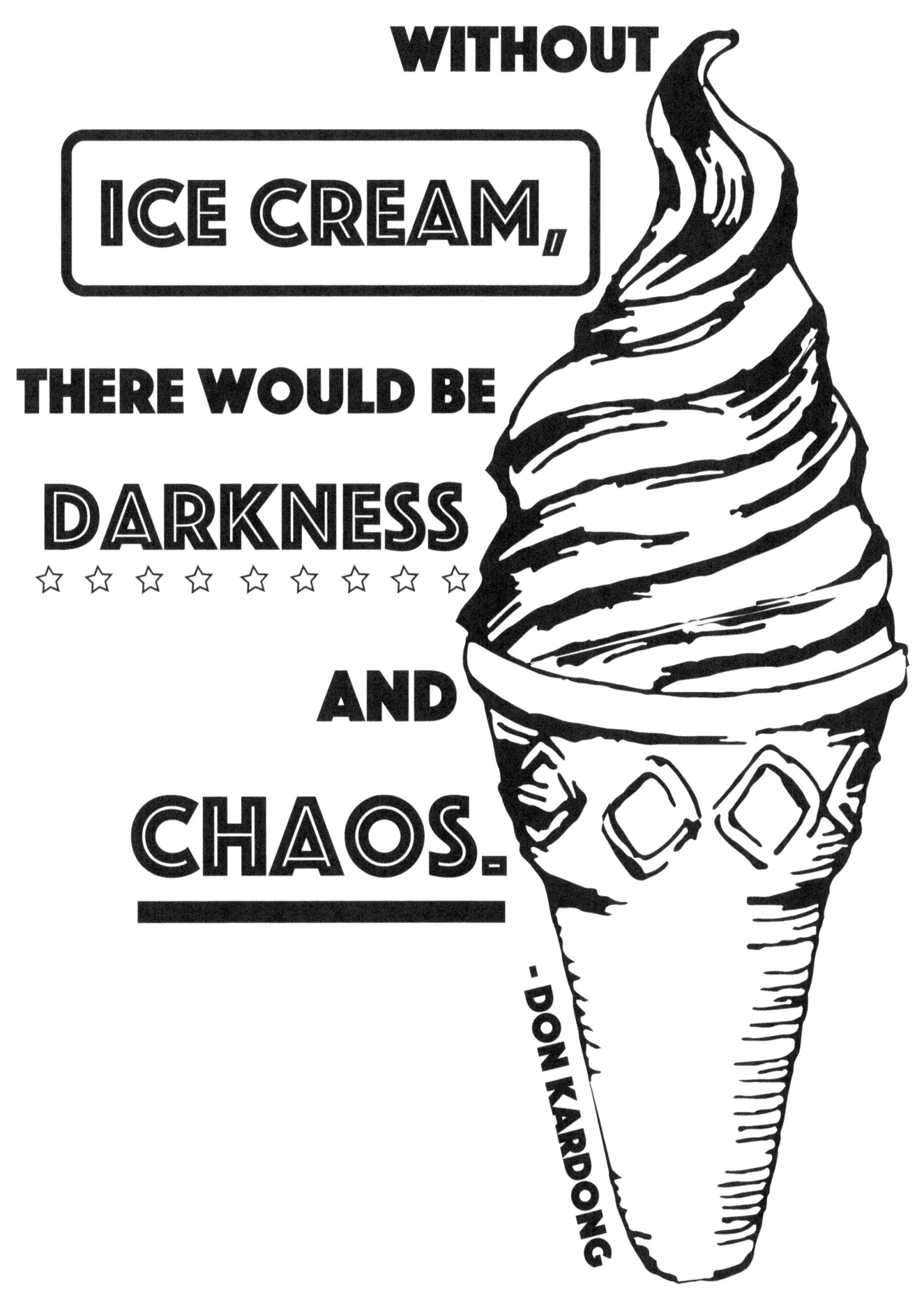

WITHOUT

ICE CREAM,

THERE WOULD BE

DARKNESS
☆☆☆☆☆☆☆☆

AND

CHAOS.

- DON KARDONG

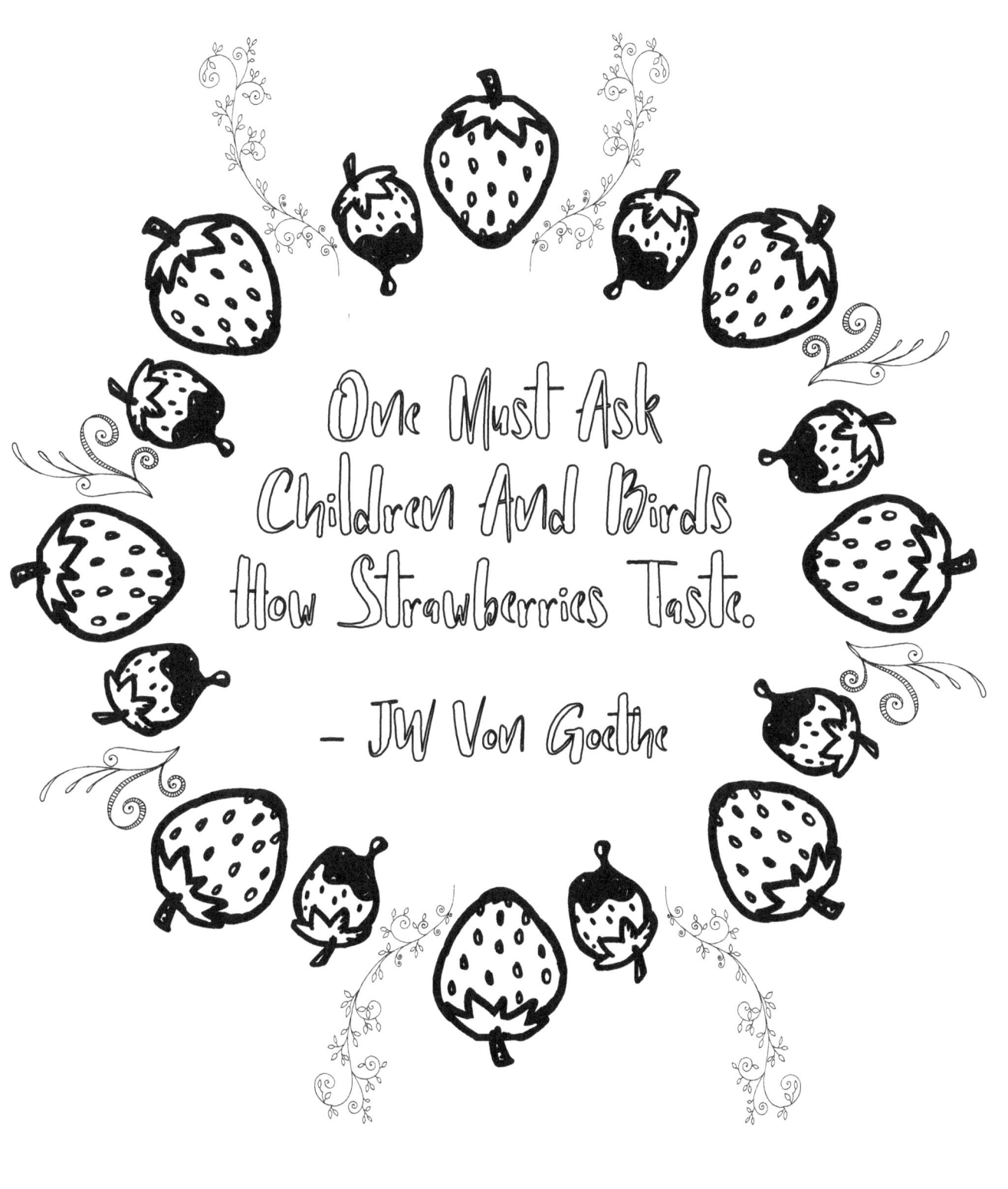

One Must Ask
Children And Birds
How Strawberries Taste.

– JW Von Goethe

MAY MY WORDS

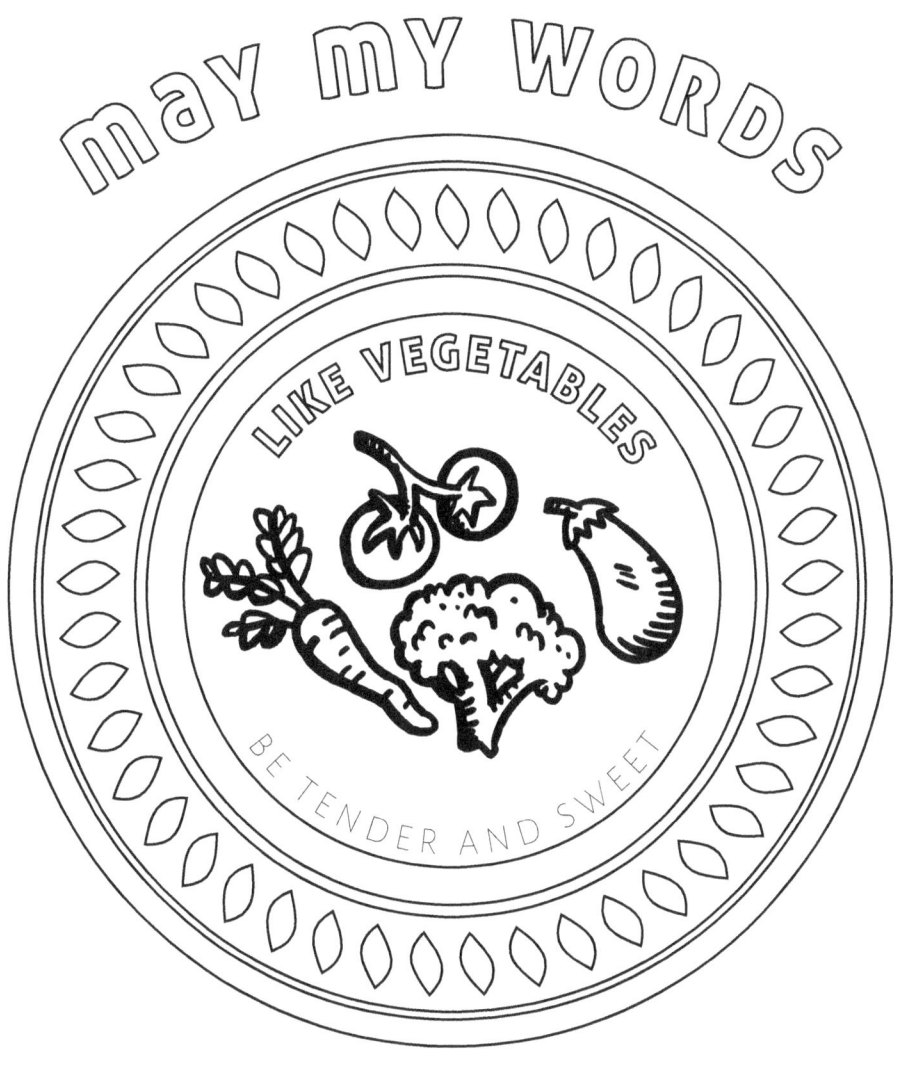

LIKE VEGETABLES

BE TENDER AND SWEET

FOR TOMORROW
I MAY HAVE
TO EAT THEM!

LIFE IS LIKE A

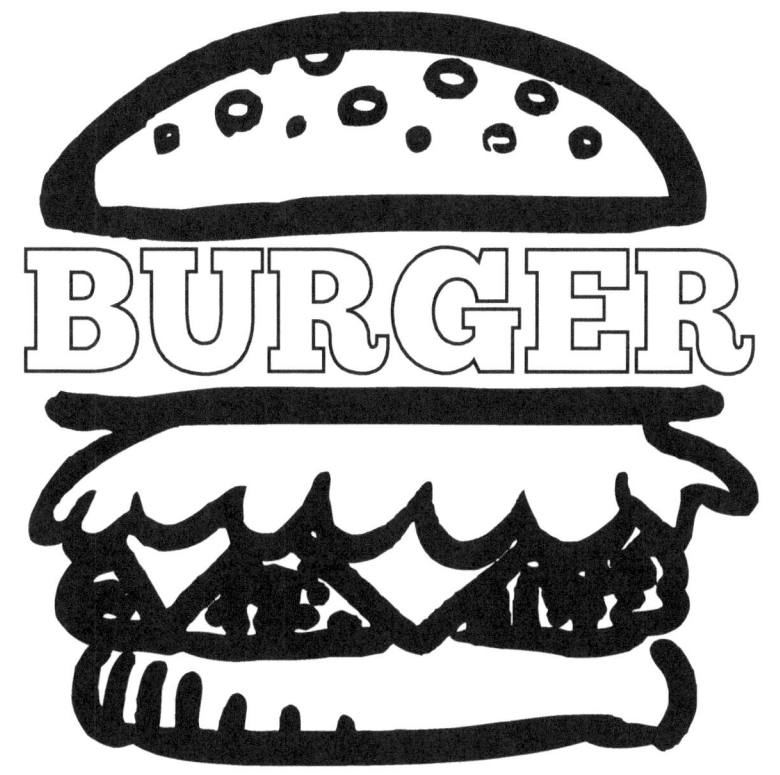

BURGER

THE MORE YOU

ADD

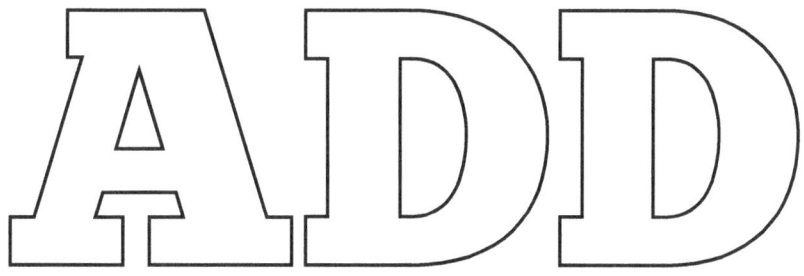

THE BETTER IT

BECOMES

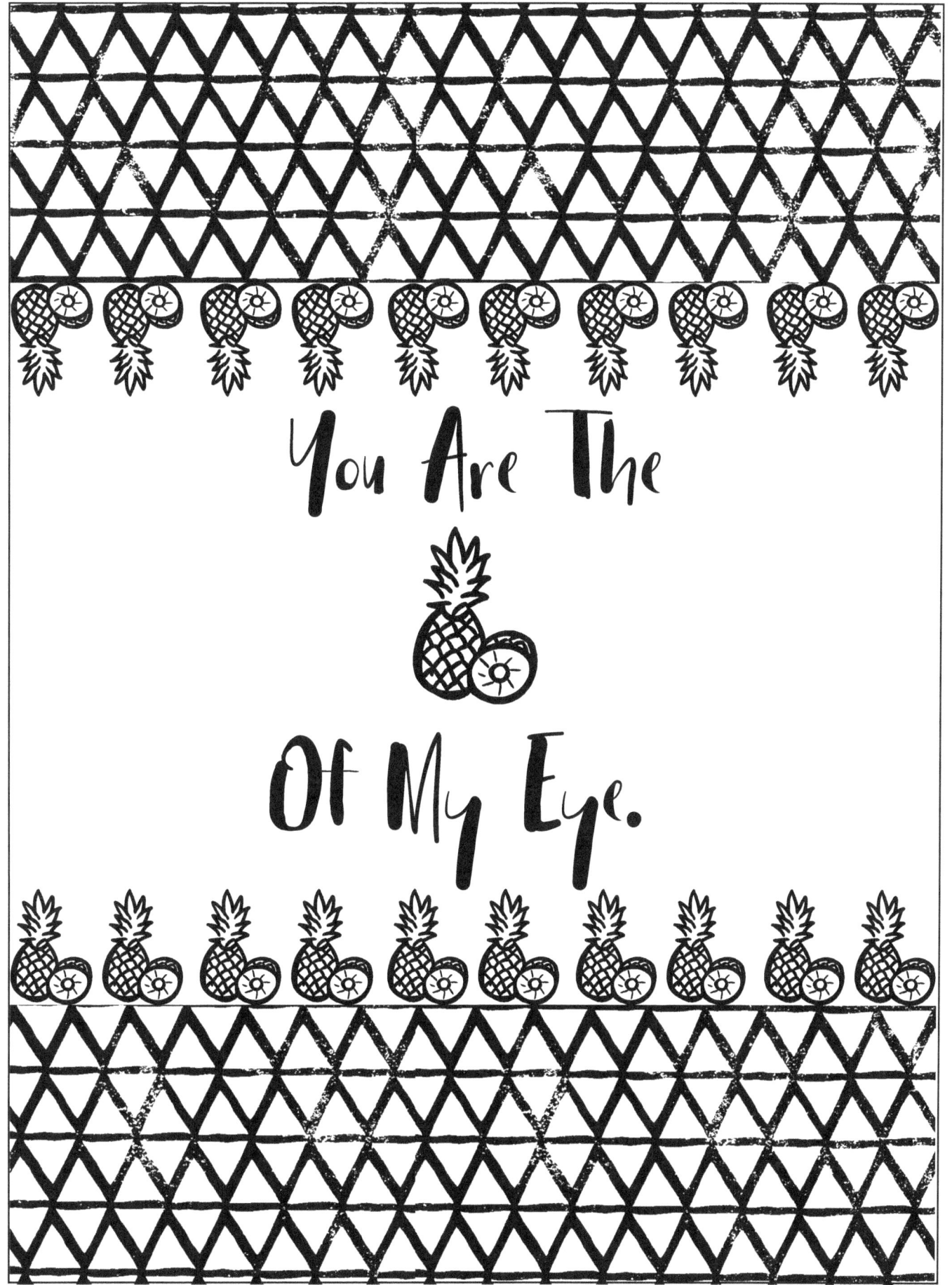

You Are The 🍍 Of My Eye.

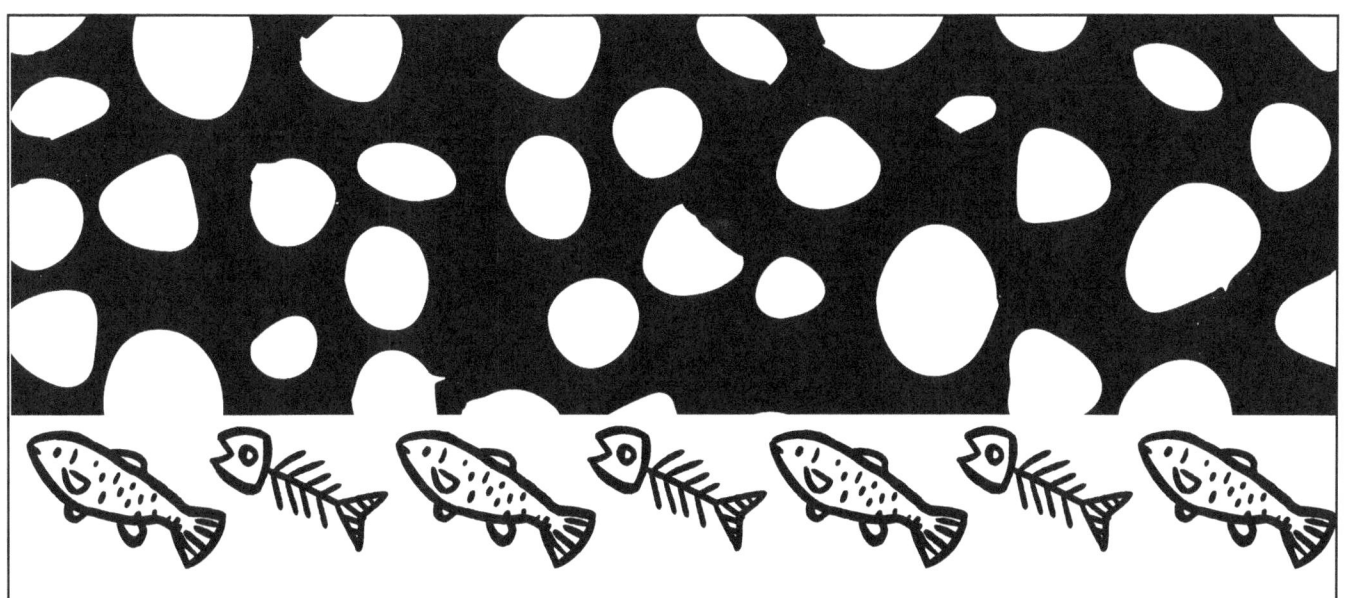

It Takes A Strong 🐟 To Swim Against The Current. Even A Dead 🐟 Can Float With It.

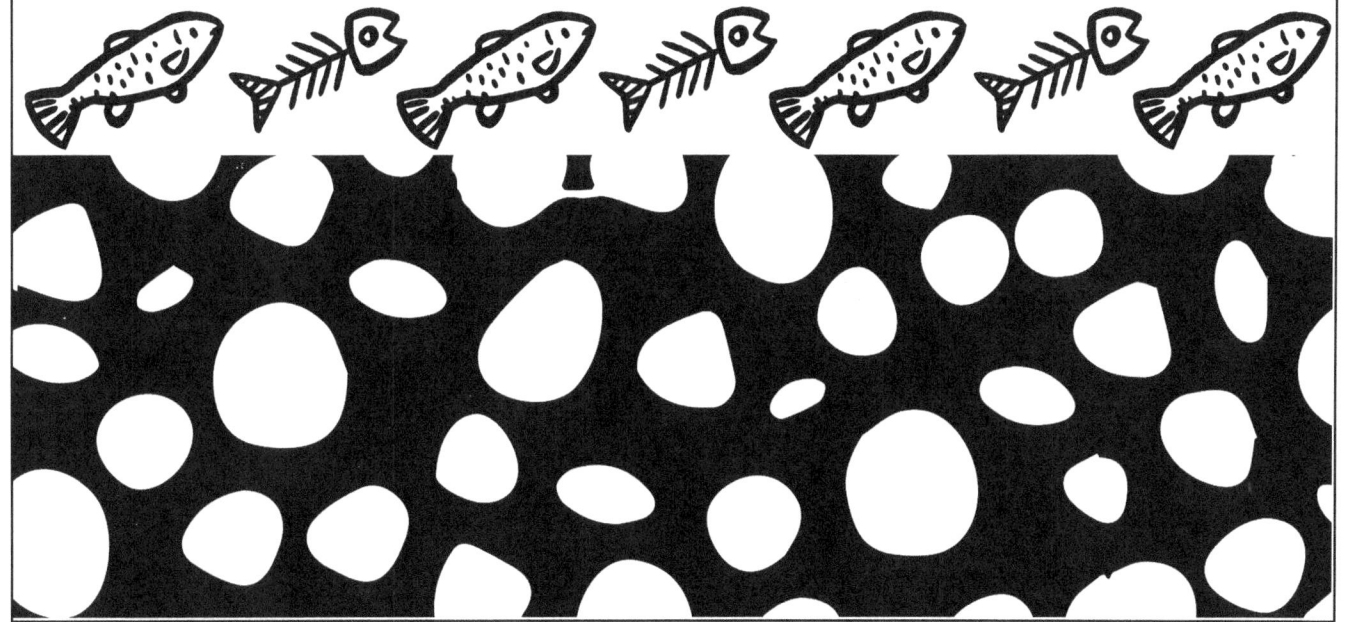

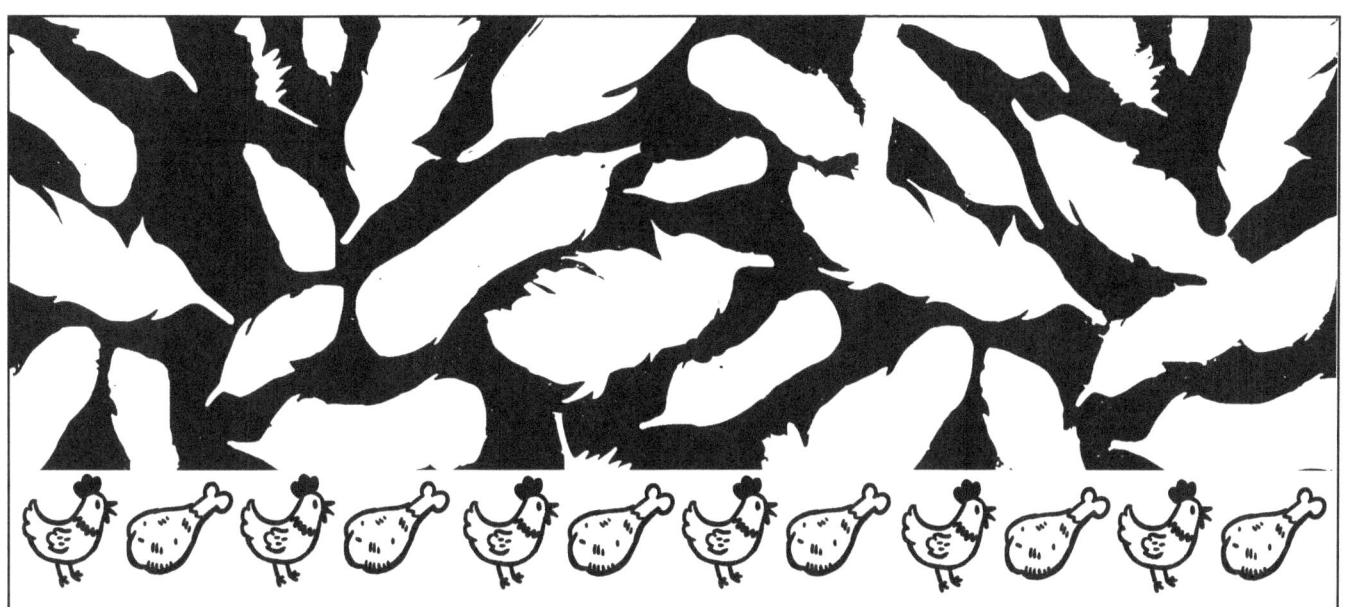

The Key To Everything Is Patience You Get The 🐔 By Hatching The 🥚 not By Smashing it.

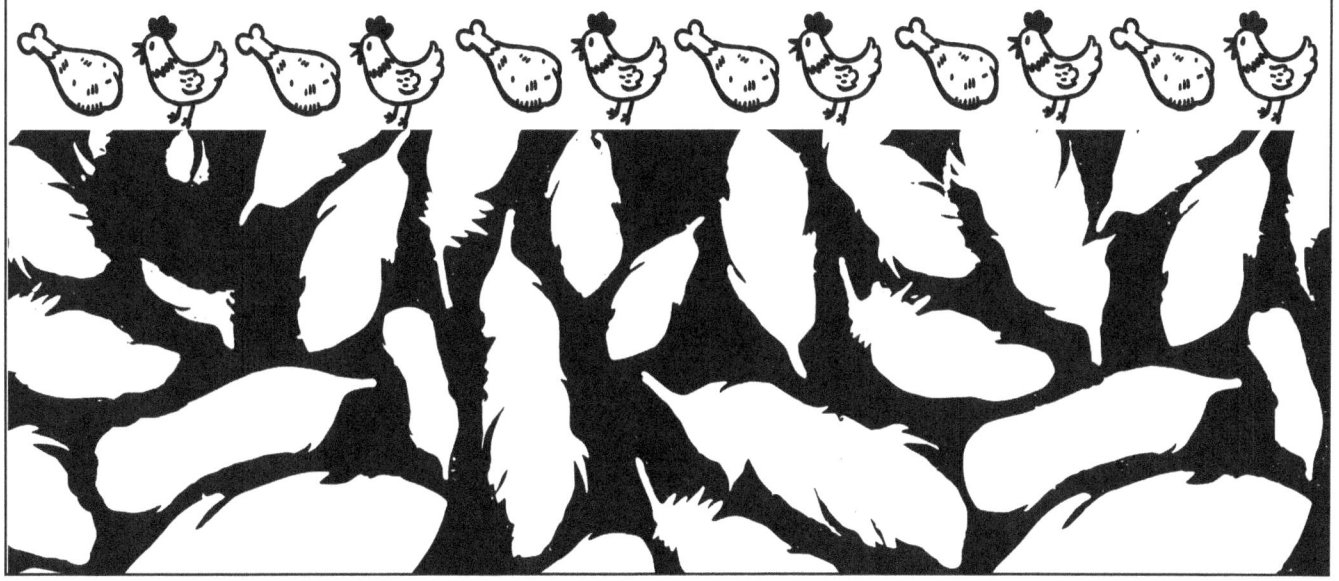

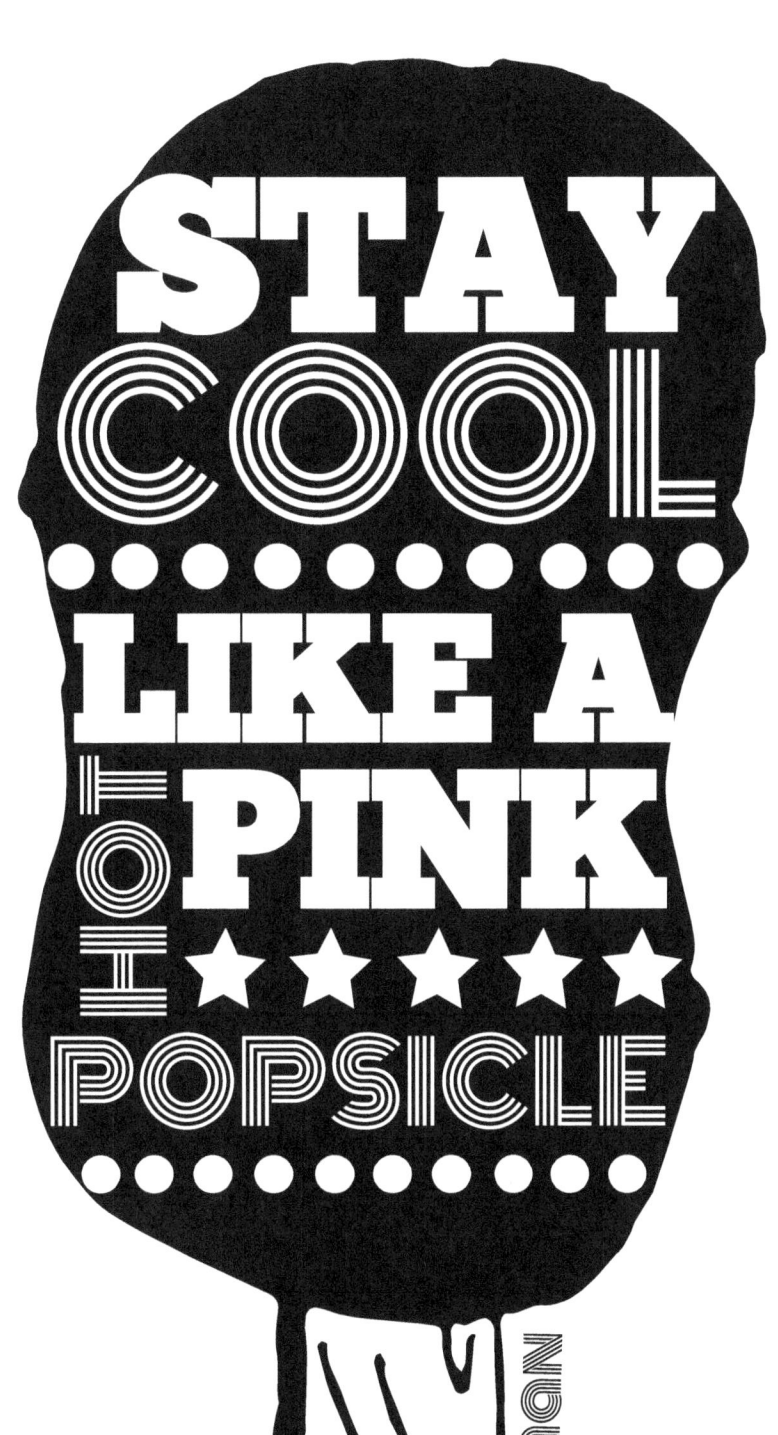

STAY COOL LIKE A HOT PINK POPSICLE

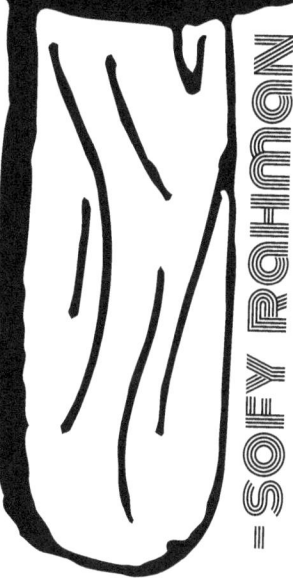

— Soify Rahman

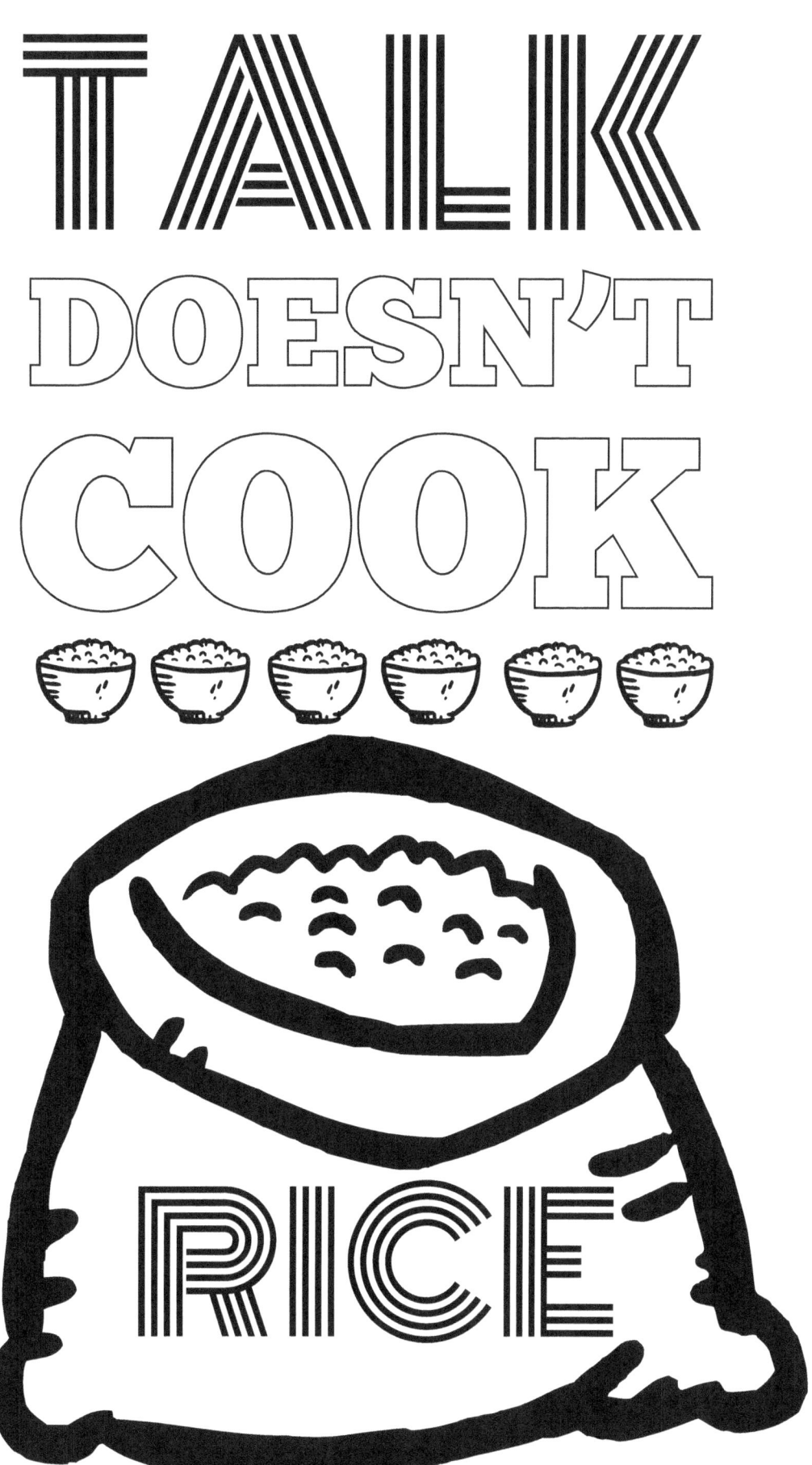

YOU ARE THE SALSA TO MY TACO

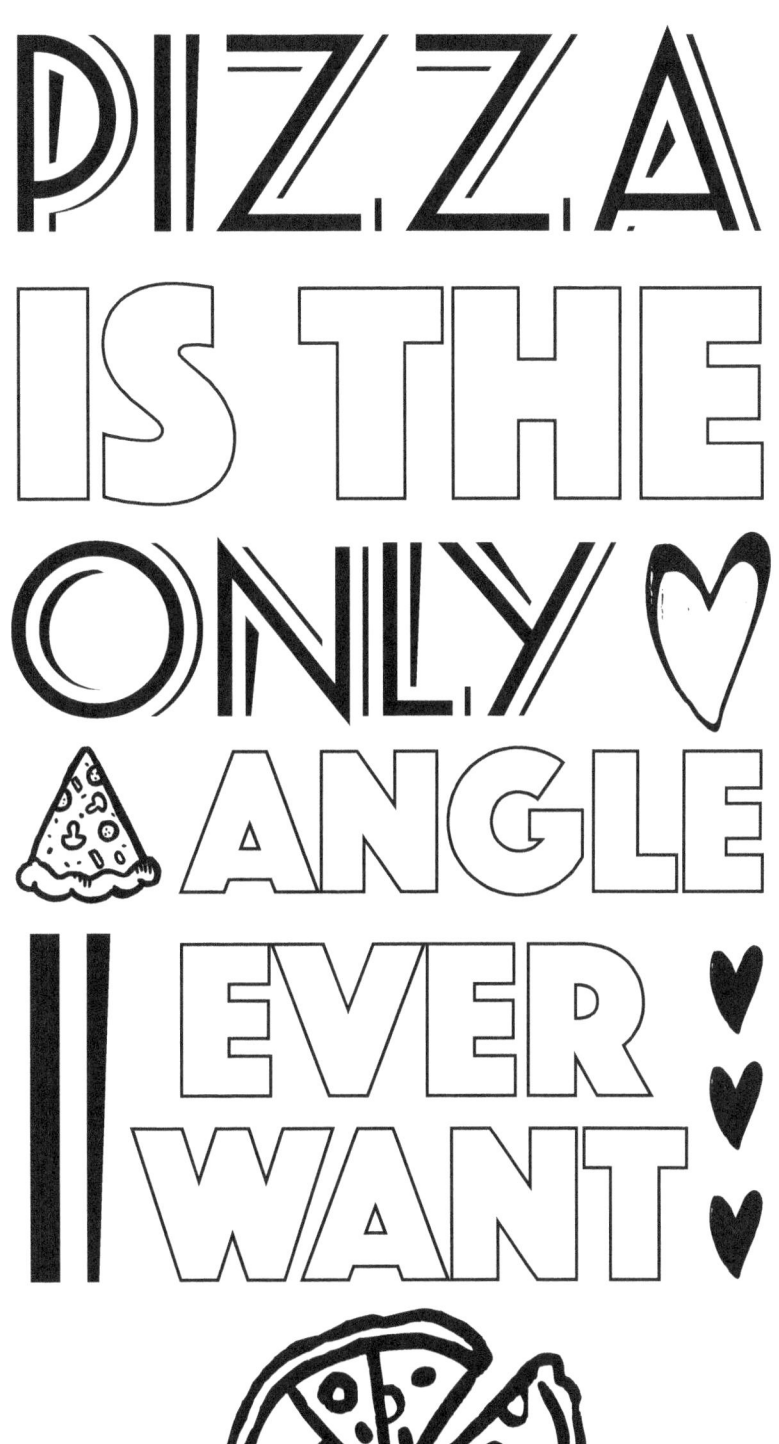

PIZZA IS THE ONLY ♡ △ ANGLE || EVER WANT

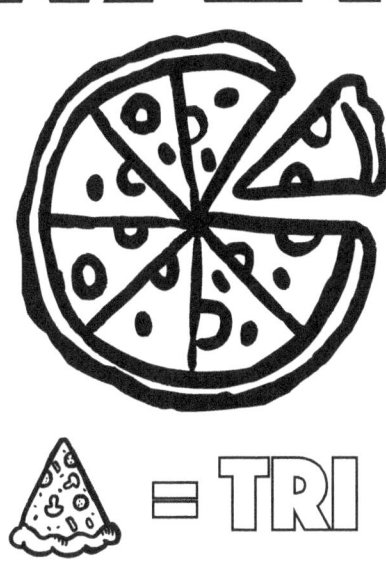

△ = TRI

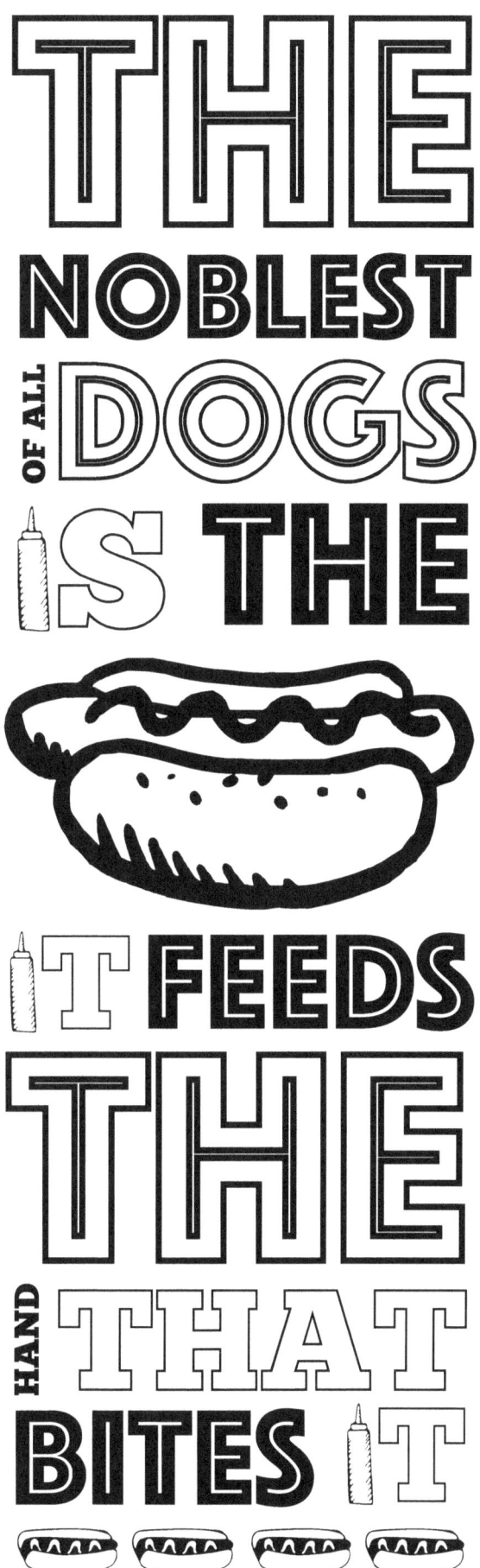

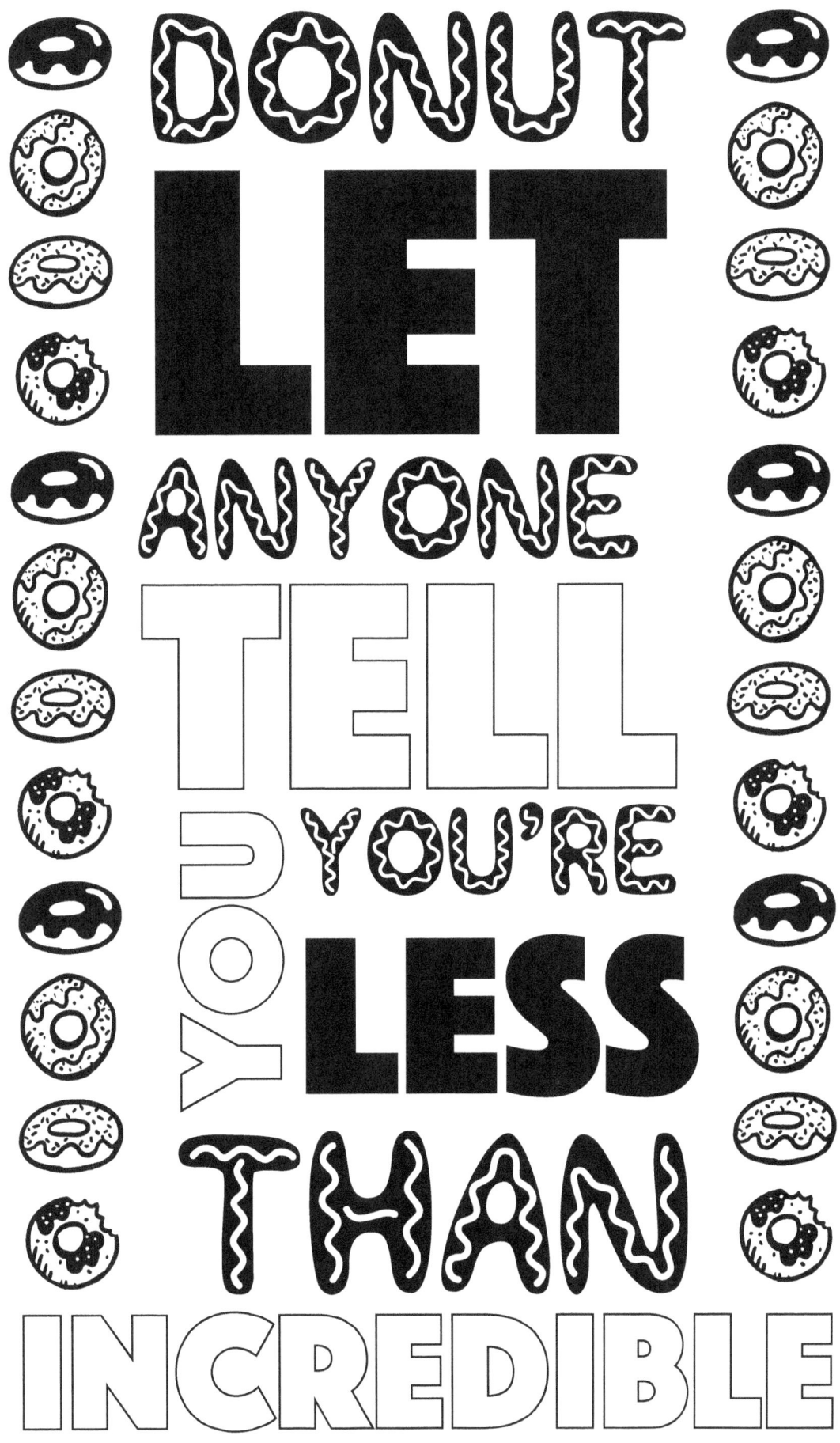

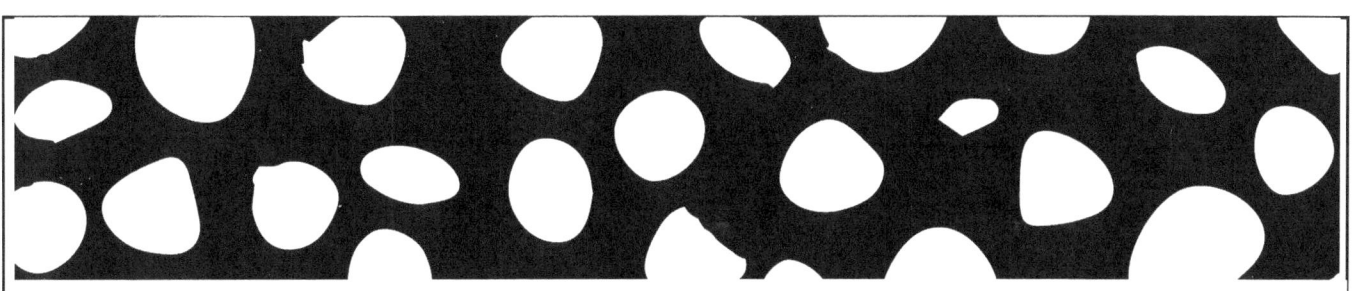

catch a man a 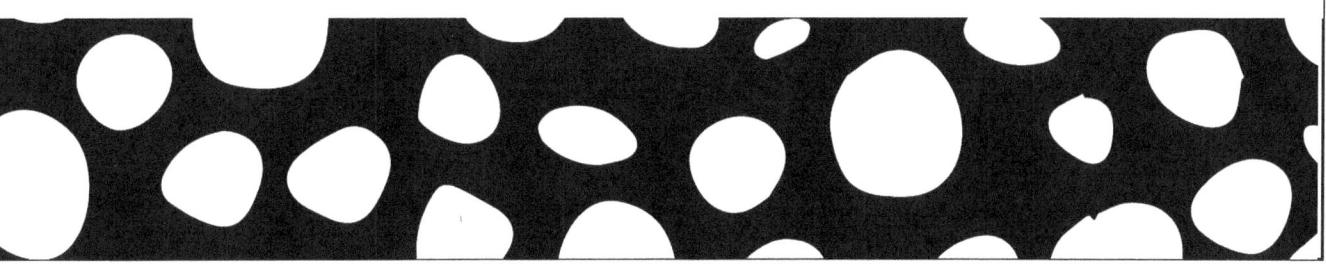,
and you can sell it to him.

teach a man to 🐟,
you ruin a wonderful
business opportunity!

life is too short

to stuff a

mushroom!